Perfect
Customer
Care

Perfect
Customer
Care

ALL YOU NEED
TO GET IT RIGHT
FIRST TIME

TED JOHNS

ARROW
BUSINESS BOOKS

Published by Arrow Books in 1994

5 7 9 10 8 6 4

First published by
Arrow Books Limited
20 Vauxhall Bridge Road, London SW1V 2SA

Random House Australia (Pty) Limited
20 Alfred Street, Milsons Point, Sydney
New South Wales 2061, Australia

Random House New Zealand Limited
18 Poland Road, Glenfield
Auckland 10, New Zealand

Random House South Africa (Pty) Limited
PO Box 337, Bergvlei, South Africa

Set in Bembo by
SX Composing Ltd., Rayleigh, Essex
Printed and bound in Great Britain by
Cox & Wyman Ltd, Reading, Berkshire

British Library Cataloguing in Publication Data
A catalogue record for this book is available from
the British Library

Random House UK Limited Reg. No. 954009

Papers used by Random House UK Limited
are natural, recyclable products made from wood grown in
sustainable forests. The manufacturing processes conform to
the environmental regulations of the country of origin.

ISBN 0–7126–5912–9

ACKNOWLEDGEMENTS

First things first. My partner, Wendy Ingram, prepared most of the manuscript for the publisher, and did an impeccable job, as she always does, against some tight deadlines.

The people who've helped me by contributing ideas and material for the book's contents, however, are the very people I can't name because of the libel laws. They're the people who make me wait in front of an empty counter (while they gossip among themselves), who hear phones ringing but don't answer them (because it's their lunch-hour), who get my name wrong, who take three weeks to reply to my letters, or who never reply at all. They're the people who never smile and who think that eye-contact is akin to rape; they make promises they have no intention of keeping; they believe that if the customer complains there is something wrong – with the customer; they cheerfully make their clients put up with behaviour which they would never tolerate if it happened to them.

I'd like to name some of these people, but my publisher tells me it would put him out of business. In any event, I can't name some of them simply because they don't have names. I assume this is the case because they don't tell me who they are, refuse to tell me who they are when I ask them, or hide behind illegible signatures.

So the best I can do is to identify some organizations which have imprinted themselves on my consciousness. This may be because their customer care is superb, a model of its kind. Alternatively, it may be because they don't yet know the meaning of the term, and at some time in the recent or distant past, they have made me suffer for their ignorance. The organizations I'm thinking about include British Airways, Prudential Assurance, the Currys/Dixons group, Forte Hotels (especially the Posthouse subsidiary), Woolworths, Safeway, BT, Malaysian Airlines, Tandy, and Southern Water. I'll leave it to you to work out whether these organizations have been named because of their excellence or because of their dross.

ABOUT THE AUTHOR

Ted Johns, PhD, MA(Soc), BSc(Econ), FIPM, ACIS, MIMC, MIMgt

For the past 26 years, Ted Johns has directed *The PROSPER Consortium*, a group of consultants specializing in the improvement of managerial performance. During part of that time he was Head of the Personnel Management Division in the Business School at Thames Valley University, where he was responsible for various post-graduate and post-experience programmes in human resource management. From 1983 onwards, Ted Johns has concentrated exclusively on his consultancy career.

Ted Johns has written five books, including **Perfect Time Management** (Century Business, 1993) and for 11 years acted as Managing Editor for the *Sundridge Park Management Review*. Current and recent consultancy and training clients have included SmithKline Beecham Consumer Brands, Philips Electronics, Pearl Assurance, Unilever, British Aerospace, the British Red Cross, and the General Electric Company (GEC). Apart from assignments in the UK, Ted Johns has designed and led training programmes on mainland Europe and in the Far East. He is a Chief Examiner for three professional bodies; he has lectured at the universities of Bradford, Kent, Sussex and Reading; his qualifications include full membership of the Institute of Management Consultants.

Ted Johns is much in demand as a keynote speaker at in-company conferences, meetings and seminars, on topics associated with time management, quality and customer care, transformational leadership, and creative innovation.

When you've read this book, you'll need first-class organization-specific training to help your organization apply the ideas, skills and techniques from these pages to the real world inhabited by your customers. The author, Ted Johns, can be contacted at PROSPER House, 30 Waterhouse Mead, Camberley, Surrey GU15 4ZD (telephone 0276-31085). It will be the best training investment you ever made.

Dr Ted Johns

CONTENTS

Dedication

To Wendy:

who knows how to generate customer delight

and also

To all those organizations which get it wrong, not just once, but day after day, revelling in their customer-service ignorance like pigs in muck

INTRODUCTION

'Customer care' is already becoming a slightly out-moded phrase and will eventually follow other phrases like 'job enrichment' and 'human relations' into oblivion. What won't descend into oblivion, however, is the need to satisfy customers. Like the drive towards quality improvement, creating customer delight is a never-ending odyssey, delivering promises to the promised land of sustainable competitive advantage.

The idea that *all* organizations have customers has burst only recently upon a stupefied and complacent world. Some have yet to acknowledge that the customer concept applies to them; some believe that it does, but they've gone alarmingly wrong in specifying who their 'customers' might be; some have embraced the notion of customer care but have done little else; some are doing their best but are rather better at talking *at* their customers than at listening *to* them. So while a few organizations lead the way, others have a lot to learn. This book is for them.

Fortunately 'customer care' is now so well established – as a money-maker for consultants, if nothing else – that we can learn from the mistakes of the path-finding pioneers. We can also benefit from the presence of impressive benchmark standards, achieved by the likes of Rank-Xerox, Kwik-Fit and even BT. As customer expectations are continually raised, we register even more powerfully the bad experiences we encounter almost every day as customers and clients, of, say, insurance companies, hotels, the transport system (in all its forms, but especially British Rail), the National Health Service and local government. Here we see, indeed, examples of organizations which still consider that they have met their customer-care obligations by answering the phone within three rings. It never seems to occur to anybody that we customers may like the person answering actually to be friendly, helpful and in-formative.

So **Perfect Customer Care** is principally targeted towards the organizations, senior managers, chief executives, middle managers and front-line customer-service staff who have barely begun to transform them-selves into customer-thinking vehicles. It makes some fairly obvious but significant points abut the import-ance of the customer, about the need to define 'custom-ers' in a way which enables us to concentrate our efforts on satisfying the people who can help us survive, and about what customers would like us to do, whatever business we're in, whatever product we make, what-ever service we provide. How customer expectations can be delivered – in strategic, tactical and operational terms – is the theme of the final chapters.

If you're in paid employment, this book is for you because you have some customers somewhere, either inside or outside your organization.

If you're self-employed, this book is for you because you must make yourself acceptable to your customers if you are to stay in business.

If you're unemployed, this book is for you because (on the assumption that you're actively looking for work) any potential employer is a 'customer' who has to be attracted and retained for as long as possible.

Whatever category you're in, simply take the concepts outlined here and translate them into your world. You've nothing to lose, everything to gain, and you can't go wrong.

WHY DOES CUSTOMER CARE MATTER?

On the face of it, this is a daft question. If you don't care for your customers, you must surely go out of business. But this isn't always the case. Here are some exceptions:

(1) **You may be competing with other organizations that don't care about their customers either.** So your customers get used to a uniformly poor and depressing level of customer service. You're only in trouble if one of your competitors suddenly raises its level of customer care and, as a result, raises the expectations of clients across the board.

(2) **You may be able to compete on factors other than customer care, like price.** Indeed, you may well believe (mistakenly, as it happens) that if you raise your level of customer service, your costs will rise and so must your prices, with the result that your sales will drop and you'll have to raise prices still further in order to sustain your cash flow. Thinking like this becomes a self-fulfilling prophecy: so long as your prices are rock-bottom and you're doing brisk business, you see no reason to change – even if it also means that your margins (and therefore your profitability) are smaller than they could be.

(3) **You may not need to compete at all if you're a monopoly.** You can treat customers with indifference, even contempt, and they will continue to come back for more because they have no option. This is the position enjoyed by the Department of

Social Security, by local authorities, and by some service functions (like personnel and training) within organizations. People employed in these functions don't even recognize that they have 'customers' at all, and their behaviour is constructed from that assumption.

(4) **You may be a solitary genius, offering products or services which are in great demand and which nobody else is yet in a position to imitate.** In a sense, therefore, you are like a monopoly supplier and as such you can afford to be arrogant: making your customers wait, giving them what you think is good for them rather than what they have asked for, even being selective about whether you accept potential customers in the first place and whether you give them the priority they seek. This kind of position is conventionally enjoyed, from time to time, by specialized computer freaks, by consultancy gurus, by film and TV directors, and so called financial wizards.

If you've just opened this book, read Chapter One so far, decided that you (or your organization) fits one of the four groups listed above, then you may be about to put the book back on the shelf, confident that it can say nothing useful to you. Before you do so, however, please take a few moments to read the next page or so, because doing so will make you uncomfortable.

The four scenarios already listed are temporary, highly dangerous and encourage complacency and inertia which lead eventually to corporate collapse or organizational decline. Why?

(1) **If you and all your competitors are indifferent to customers, and therefore aren't really competing at all, what happens if one of them suddenly does seek to create a competitive advantage through a reputation for customer**

service (for example, Kwik-Fit in the tyre market)? All the time you continue to act as before, you will be left behind as your innovative rival grabs market share. This process can continue, moreover, so long as customer care continues to be the competitive edge, until you are bought out or finally surrender. And should you think this could never happen, because your competitors are as sleepy as you are, don't be so sure. Somebody, somewhere, will eventually wake up to the benefits of customer care as a hugely cost-effective Unique Selling Proposition. It may be somebody who picks up a book like this one and starts to think about its potential applications, somebody who's learnt about positive customer service on the receiving end of Marks & Spencer, or somebody who absorbs the messianic messages of customer service while they're at college. What you can be certain of, in an uncertain world, is that it's going to happen sometime.

(2) **Competing solely on price is based on the assumption that cost is the dominant, or even the only, factor in purchasing decisions, whether made by individuals or by organizations.** The evidence completely contradicts this belief. Virtually every survey of consumer motivation puts price *below* other critical factors like quality, 'value-for-money', courteous service, and rapid availability. Obviously there are exceptions, but it's worth noting that in most fields of commercial endeavour (for example, retail foods), companies that compete on price alone have not been conspicuously successful when contrasted with those that mingle price with other significant features of the marketing mix. It is equally clear

that price is only one element in corporate purchasing decisions. Clearly, if other factors are held constant, then a price advantage may be crucial in securing business – but it is rare, very rare, for other factors to be constant when price sinks to rock-bottom levels. To illustrate our point, here's one recent study of the factors influencing corporate purchasing decisions among head-office buyers for a major UK food product group:

Hierarchy of Customer Service Elements Among Head Office Buyers (UK Food Group)	
1. Product availability	7. Pricing
2. Prompt quotation	8. Merchandising
3. Representatives	9. Product positioning
4. Order status	10. Invoice accuracy
5. Distribution system	11. New products
6. Delivery time	12. Advertising

(3) **You may be a monopoly now, but will you be one for ever?** The British economy is littered with examples of organizations that have suddenly found themselves exposed to competitive conditions: 'market testing' in government departments, airports, electricity supply, and the like. Nowadays it is much more common for internal service functions to compete for 'contracts' with external agencies, especially in such fields as in-house catering, training, and corporate transport facilities.

Some were prepared for the change, or adapted rapidly to the new situation, and some weren't or didn't. The degree of suffering has been directly proportional to the complacency and inertia with which some organizations have confronted their open-market scenario, given that monopoly (or quasi-monopoly) is almost invariably associated with high costs, high prices, overmanning, an introspective mentality and an indifference to the external world (especially 'customers'). Even if you do enjoy a monopoly position today, it surely makes strategic sense to act as if you don't, in order to pre-empt antagonism, and delay what you might undoubtedly regard as the 'evil day' when you actually do face the real world. This may seem like good advice, but it's never been heeded by some organizations especially those in transportation, that have sought to kill their competition at every turn so that they can return to their comfortable security of single-supplier status once more.

(4) **OK, so you're a genius.** You can afford to be temperamental, an ego-maniac, awkward, aggressive, domineering – *but only so long as your genius is in demand*. And if you're too obnoxious, your clients will look elsewhere for more amenable substitutes. So arrogance carries the seeds of its own destruction. Being difficult, moreover, is a two-edged weapon because it's likely to mean that your customers become more difficult, too: things take longer to happen, clients are mysteriously unavailable, invoices are challenged. By being difficult you end up making your own life difficult, and where's the benefit in that?

CUSTOMER CARE IS IMPORTANT FOR EVERYBODY

So far we've argued that whoever you are, whatever you do, concern for your customers is a vital ingredient in your success, effectiveness and future prosperity. Let's go on to make a few more assumptions.

1. **Everybody does have 'customers'.** Some people

believe that customer care doesn't apply to them because they don't have customers – and they probably don't, if the word 'customer' is used in its old-fashioned, restrictive and traditional sense. However, if we extend the definition of 'customer' to cover the people for whom you provide a service, whether inside or outside the organization, then the concept is much clearer. Using this approach, the people in the next department to yours are your 'customers', as are (if you are in an internal service role) the line managers who come to you for advice and assistance, or the project manager for whose team you supply an input. It makes good sense to regard your boss as your customer, too, especially if he complains about the quality of service you give him.

2. **Customer care isn't enough.** For many people and organizations nowadays, a high standard of quality and customer care is taken for granted. Customer service, in other words, is a necessary but not a sufficient condition of competitive survival: to stay in business, you must pay attention to your customers, but doing so will not give you a sustainable advantage against your competitors, especially as customer–service practices can be easily imitated. If one company (Kwik-Fit) introduces a telephone hotline to its managing director so that complaints (and compliments) can get quickly to the top, then other companies in the same field of business (or even in other businesses) can instantly do the same. Reading this book, and acting on it, won't guarantee that you and your business will prosper because other things matter as well:

- *Even if your customer care is brilliant, you must still have a product or service that people want or need.*
- *Your customers must also be prepared to pay for the product or service you are offering.* Although price is only

one factor in the customer's mix of decision elements, as it were, it may be that the price being charged for whatever you have on offer is prohibitive and therefore you lose customers. This is all the more depressing if you personally aren't responsible for fixing the price.

- *Whereas excellence in customer care was once a relevant offensive strategy for grabbing extra market share, it's increasingly a defensive necessity.*

Some salutary stories: how to do it, and how not to do it

1. *General Motors and Nissan.* General Motors was having trouble with a supplier of car seats whose quality was persistently deficient. One day a couple of GM executives attended a conference at which a speaker from Nissan referred to the excellence of the company's seat supplier. *It was the same company that GM was having trouble with.*

Both 'customers' (GM and Nissan) had provided the supplier with a specification, but only Nissan gave regular, detailed feedback about problems.

Moral: Performance can only improve if customers complain.

2. *Xerox Copiers.* At one time, Xerox had the copier market to itself. But, as Joseph Juran writes, 'There was a snake in this paradise. Its machines were failure-prone. You became very well acquainted with the people who came in to service the machines. So Xerox set up a service department. That solved the problem so far as the company was concerned, but not for the customers.'

The failures continued, and Xerox had to decide whether to redesign the machines to eliminate the failures or increase the size of the service force. They took the latter option, recruiting more service personnel and making a significant profit from the service function. Logically, the product design and manufacturing departments now had no incentive to improve the built-in quality of the copiers because to have done so would have reduced the workload (and therefore the profitability) of the service area.

Sensing a flaw in this cosy arrangement, competitors (especially from Japan, and notably Canon) came out with new copiers that did not fail. In the small machine sector they took the market away from Xerox.

Yet arguably the different parts of Xerox were doing their jobs well, albeit in a compartmentalized, inward-looking, short-sighted fashion. Certainly the factory was producing acceptable copiers, and the service function was supplying speedy and efficient service whenever anything went wrong. The only trouble was that the external customers weren't happy, and ultimately they had the opportunity to articulate that unhappiness by taking their custom elsewhere.

Moral: Customer service is **efficient** if it means putting things right which have gone wrong; customer service is **effective** if the product is right first time. To put it another way: the best kind of customer service isn't even noticed by the customer because it happens before the product/service even reaches the customer.

3. *Procter and Gamble.* When P&G opened a direct phone line for consumers, they handled thousands of calls each month. Only about 20 per cent referred to the taste of the toothpaste or the whiteness created by the washing powder. Eighty per cent of complaints were about seemingly peripheral issues: boxes, handles, tube-tops, colours and typefaces.

Similarly, a Swedish study has found that only 17 per cent of customer problems were concerned with whether the product or service worked as claimed. Instead, the vast majority of problems reflected criticism about what may have seemed to be less significant dimensions, like delivery or packaging.

Moral: The majority of customer complaints will not directly relate to the quality of the service/product, but to the peripheral issues. Quality in the eyes of the customer is always supposedly much more than the quality of the product or basic service offered. In judging how well the product/service meets his needs, the customer wraps everything into one:

- Product/service reliability
- Consistency
- Speed and timeliness of delivery
- Accuracy of paperwork
- Courtesy of telephone answering
- Value of information given (e.g. product/service user instructions)
- Reputation of the delivering organization
- Positive attitude by staff

All these elements are important, and some are critical. The only reliable way to find out is to look and listen, and to supply positive opportunities for giving feedback: surveys help, but don't provide real, understanding.

4. *Tourism in the former USSR.* This story is told by a marketing expert specializing in tourism, who was advising a Soviet resort on how to attract more Western visitors. He had a long, fruitless discussion with the tourism officials; every suggestion he made was greeted with obstacles and difficulties. If he argued that bicycles

should be rented to young holiday-makers, the Russians insisted that this could not be done 'because it would be too dangerous.'

At last one of the Soviets said, 'Visitors to the Soviet Union have got to realize . . . '

The consultant interrupted. 'Just a minute. A tourist does not have to realize anything. A tourist sits in Manchester or Manhattan and chooses a two-week holiday. The choice is no different from a decision over motor cars or meals.'

Moral: The problems of the manufacturer or the chef are not the problems of the consumer. Customers are not interested in your shortage of staff, the fact that the computer has gone down, power cuts, rail strikes, leaves on the line, frozen points, portion control policies and practices, your need for a lunch-break. If the customer isn't interested in these things, don't bother telling him about them. First he will be bored, and then angry. Serves you right.

5. *The US carpet company.* One of the company's European customers came up with its own test for the carpet foam backing, but the company told the customer not to bother with its own test: 'We already measure for foam stability, molecular weight distribution, particle size conformity, per cent of unreacted monomer, adhesion strength' and so on, 'so you're getting the best there is – real quality.' Yet the customer returned the goods three times, claiming that 'your product can't pass my roll-stool test.' What the customer was doing was placing a weight on the bottom half of an office chair (under-carriage and castors), and spinning it round on a piece of test carpet 30,000 times. The sample failed the test if the carpet delaminated from the foam backing.

Eventually the manufacturer was persuaded to use the same test himself and gave the customer a product which could withstand 80,000 spins before delaminating.

Moral: Quality (and customer service) is what the customer says it is, not what your internal guidelines (or tests) indicate is satisfactory.

6. *US car makers and the Japanese market.* This story, with a moral similar to that of the US carpet company cited above, is taken from *Mass Customization: The New Frontier in Business Competition* by B Joseph Pine II (Boston: Harvard University Press, 1993). American car manufacturers have long complained about the 'intractability' of the Japanese market, arguing that it is impossible to gain any significant market share because of Japanese industrial and government practices. However, it became clear in 1992 that despite some truth in the claim, it was also the case that Detroit had done little to meet the requirements of potential customers in Japan. Because the Japanese drive on the left, they position the steering wheel on the right. Japanese automobile companies have always produced right-hand steering for their domestic market and left-hand steering for exports to the USA and other appropriate countries. That degree of flexibility has apparently been too much for Detroit, who have persisted in trying to compel the Japanese to buy a product without even the most elementary features relevant to the Japanese situation. In response to questions on this issue during President George Bush's January 1992 trip to Japan, when he was accompanied by some senior automobile executives, the CEO of Ford remarked:

'You've got a market of 6.8 million units in Japan, the imports total 2.9 per cent. That says something about the

Japanese market. All the manufacturers in the world can't be that bad ... The cars we sell from the US have left-hand drive. But would right-hand drive really make a big difference? A lot of manufacturers have right-hand capability, but look at those total imports into Japan. Right-hand drive alone won't make that much difference.'

Moral: If the obvious needs of the customer are ignored, then the less-obvious requirements have no chance.

7. *US carmakers and the American market.* When the trend towards smaller cars began in 1969, the response of the American automakers was not to build small cars, but rather to sell more aggressively whatever they happened to be making. As the president of General Motors said that year, 'Never has the need for aggressive salesmanship and good management been more critical.' Five years later, when it became obvious that consumers were moving away in droves from large (American) automobiles to smaller (Japanese) models, the response of the chairman of GM was the same: 'We've got a selling job to do with the dealer, and he has a job to do with the customer.' B Joseph Pine II observes:

'The job of [automobile] salespersons, as with all mass producers, is not to figure out what the customer wants so much as to sell what the manufacturer has already built ... dealers ... pushed prospective customers to forgo desired options that were not on the floor models, and to accept options on the floor models that they would have preferred to do without. A sales general manager retiring from one of the automakers said with pride, "If I've accomplished nothing else in my years, I have succeeded in stamping out special orders!"'

Moral: Hard-sell tactics used to sell lower-quality, less-innovative goods (or services) that are not what the customer wants will lead to disgruntled and disloyal customers. People will only tolerate hard-sell tactics if they end up with something they really want. If what they purchase turns out to be not quite what they want, then their dissatisfaction with the product or service is magnified by their dissatisfaction with the sales tactics. Note the contrast between the US carmakers on the one hand, and Toyota on the other. Toyota's consistent marketing strategy has emphasized variety, customization and individuality, paradoxically within a mass-production context, in order to satisfy the increasingly idiosyncratic expectations of its customers. Today, Toyota offers five-day delivery of custom-ordered cars in Japan – and this is by no means the limit of its potential.

8. *British Airways*. In 1983 British Airways intensified its market research, trying to establish exactly what it was that made passengers elect to fly a particular airline again – repeat purchase being a significant factor in airline revenue. In the event, the research identified a number of salient features of service for its major passenger segments:

- For relatively inexperienced VFR (Visiting Friends and Relations) passengers, anxiety reduction was paramount
- For holiday-makers and tourists, the keys were glamour, champagne and excitement
- For the experienced and jaundiced business traveller on short haul, the needs were described as 'rational' – a timely arrival, special communication facilities in the event of unavoidable delays, and so forth.

Although the study was quite sophisticated, it failed to perceive one potentially salient feature for the business traveller. For in the spring of 1983 British Midland introduced the breakfast sausage to early-morning internal flights, and businessmen switched carriers in vast numbers. *The added value was the sausage.* BA responded within months by introducing the Super Shuttle; its dominance was re-established; but British Midland retained its deserved reputation as an aggressive, imaginative innovator.

Moral: Market research is of limited value in helping you to improve customer service, because it can only give you answers to the questions you ask, and customers can only tell you about the needs they know about. What customers can't do is tell you about the needs they don't even know they have – until you supply something that activates a previously unknown want, a want that from then on becomes indispensable and whose satisfaction your competitors have to match.

9. *The Tennant Company (US floor maintenance equipment maker).* In his book *Thriving on Chaos* (London: Macmillan, 1988), Tom Peters describes what happened when Doug Hoelscher, a Tennant vice-president, phoned the president of his largest supplier. 'I was apprehensive about calling the president to tell him that there "might be" some quality-related problems with his product that he "might not" know about. His response: "Why the hell are you calling *me*? I have people to handle these kinds of things." I took a deep breath and explained that at Tennant Company we were trying a new approach. We wanted to become more involved with our counterparts in key supplier companies, and we had set a goal of reducing our supplier base by ten per cent a year over the next five years. I seemed to have his attention. I said I hoped he was interested in keeping our business and invited him to a meeting.

'We showed him documentation outlining the percentage of parts received from his company that we had to reject. It became obvious to him that the product he was selling was not of the quality his people had led him to believe. "What do you want me to do?" he asked.

'We explained that we had three requirements: set annual improvement goals; meet with us annually to review progress; become a fully qualified supplier by meeting these goals ... The result has been a much more satisfactory relationship. His company did set and meet goals. It is one of our group of major suppliers.'

Moral: If you're a senior person, it's reasonable to assume that accurate information about quality standards and customer-service performance is being withheld from you. The only way to overcome this is for you to get out among your customers yourself, find out firsthand, and challenge your own people.

10. *Customer service: why the gap between promise and performance?* Many other books on customer care, quality and customer service will tell you glowing stories about what supposedly reputable, large and benchmark organizations have done in the field of customer service: how much they've spent on training, the gimmicks they've used to enhance customer-service performance, the rewards they offer to those of their staff who implement (and preferably exceed) prescribed standards. For instance, Sarah Cook's *Customer Care* (London: Kogan Page, 1992) contains impressive accounts about such companies as National Westminster Bank, Lloyds Bank, Midland Bank, British Rail, Comet, Thames Water, British Gas and the Nationwide Building Society. Vast sums have been spent as if throwing money at the problem will solve it: British Airways' 'Putting People First' programme is alleged to have cost

some £23 million; the Royal Bank of Scotland has spent £2 million on customer-care training; at a more modest level, the Woolwich Building Society programme for its 3,500 employees cost £80 a head, or a total of £280,000.

It doesn't do to appear hypercritical, but there has been remarkably little to show for all the time, effort, planning, organization and money poured into customer-service 'improvements', at least so far as some organizations are concerned. All right, perhaps the most spectacular example of a customer-care programme being credited for improved business performance is British Airways, which, from being a loss-maker in the early 1980s, made a profit of £176 million and was named 'Airline of the Year' in 1985 following implementation of its 'Putting People First' campaign. Yet the causes of BA's financial improvement could be laid at the door of other factors, or causes additional to improved customer service; and even if BA had a customer-care competitive advantage in 1985, it has not been successful in retaining its lead thereafter.

Far more widespread is a feeling of incredulity on learning that some organizations have gone through an intensive customer-service-enhancement drive. If so, where are the results? Maybe there have been higher standards of achievement, dissipated because they haven't kept pace with more sophisticated expectations among customers themselves. But what is the point of improving customer service if it still lags behind what customers want, need and expect?

The possible reasons for the discrepancy between intention and accomplishment will be explored in greater depth elsewhere in this book, together with some suggestions for avoiding the problem. To cover the issues briefly here, however, it seems that when customer-care programmes fail to deliver the goods, the most probable causes are:

(a) A superficial, propaganda-style approach in which it is assumed that, say, a half-day course in telephone techniques will produce miracles across the board.

(b) An apparent belief that the mere dissemination of mission statements and customer charters will be sufficient in itself to transform rank-and-file behaviour.

(c) Lack of commitment, or mere lip-service commitment, from the top.

(d) A contradiction between the loudly trumpeted messages about the importance of customers, and the reality of meagre resources and hostile attitudes.

(e) A failure to train customer-interface personnel in elementary interpersonal skills (other than through glib platitudes).

(f) Centralized (and therefore slow) decision-making when confronting customer complaints.

(g) So-called 'training' which takes the form of messianic messages rather than practical problem-solving.

(h) The absence of any reward or recognition system aimed at customer-care standards.

(i) No attention to the recruitment of front-line customer-service personnel with the basic attributes for dealing with people.

(j) Reluctance to 'empower' staff so that they can use their initiative when dealing with dissatisfied customers.

11. *Airlines*. A *Daily Telegraph* feature on customer care included optimistic notes about an airline's new

customer care service – significantly, a permanently manned telephone line, something of an innovation, apparently – and the resulting 94 per cent increase in the volume of incoming calls for the customer-relations department. We were told that:

'The staff has moved to light, airy offices, with the deliberate intention of putting them at the hub of the organization rather than being tucked away in a dark corner where companies tend to relegate their complaints department.'

Of course, the light, airy offices could still have been tucked away in a light, airy corner, but let's put cynicism on one side for a moment. We learn that directors 'may be found spending evenings and weekends personally telephoning aggrieved customers, who are sometimes a little surprised to get a call from a senior executive.' Furthermore, customer relations staff who receive complaints or suggestions will pass them on to those responsible in a 'caring' way, adopting a 'mature discussion approach' rather than a finger-wagging ticking–off.

All this sounds superb and wonderful, but it suffers from two powerful disadvantages. First, customer relations concentrates on handling *complaints*, that is, it tries to put right things that have already gone wrong, or apologize and offer refunds (if you're lucky). Secondly, by definition customer relations here are primarily remedial: for every ten positive improvements it is instrumental in introducing, it will suffer from single incidents of poor customer service between cabin service staff and 'customers' (= passengers). The impact of these incidents is made worse if the victim happens to have access to the media.

Thus a national newspaper recently carried some acerbic observations about a trans-European flight 'enjoyed' by one of its principal feature writers. The article referred to lousy food, long waits for service, irritating announcements and a very obvious contempt for 'steerage' passengers.

A foreign woman had asked for something from the drinks trolley and been spoken to very rudely by the stewardess. The passengers were subjected to various messages transmitted over the public address system by the head of the cabin crew; after the flight was over the journalist sought him out to complain, receiving the response "You'll just have to write to the marketing director then, won't you?"

'Moments of truth' like this can certainly put paid to the sterling efforts of customer service people in their light, airy offices. And why is it that, whenever a group of globe-trotting business people gather together, the conversation will quickly turn, competitively, to the latest tortures inflicted on them by various airlines? These may well include the slowness of any response generated by the customer relations department, or the absence of any response at all, or self-serving complaints by the customer service telephonists about the volume of work they are expected to process (which raises the interesting dilemma: who do people in a customer-complaints department complain to?).

Moral: It's better to spend lots of money on genuine up-front customer-service improvements than on PR window dressing which doesn't fool anyone, least of all customers who themselves are in the PR business.

12. *The financial services sector*. The airline saga illustrates the dangers that companies run when they play fast and loose with customers (or their agents) who turn out to be communication gatekeepers with the opportunity to broadcast corporate shortcomings to a much larger audience. In this way a major company in financial services fell foul of a journalist who writes on consumer protection. A correspondent had suffered some bad experiences in the hands of an insurance company and had written to the newspaper on the matter, closing his letter with the rhetorical question, 'What on earth can one do with such an awful company?'

The journalist's response suggested that the company was 'depressingly comatose'. Having contacted the company on seven separate occasions, both in writing and by telephone, he had received no written reply, and no telephone call had been returned.

On one occasion a responsible official had promised that the matter would be attended to immediately, but nothing happened.

Even when the company knew they were dealing with a journalist it made no difference.

Moral: You can't afford to be cavalier with any customer. Another moral of this story is: There's no point in making lots of noise about customer service, and spending money on customer care, if you then treat your employees with such contempt that they undermine your objectives by stealth.

13. *Rank Xerox – again*. Let's bring the chapter to an end with some happier material. As we've seen, at the end of the 1970s 'the Japanese were killing the company' (to quote Vern Zelmer, the UK's managing director).

Since then the company has turned itself round, not least because of its powerful adherence to quality. Mr Zelmer has been quoted as saying, however, that quality standards such as BS5750 do not quite fit the bill because they deal with procedures, not processes, and overlook the importance of looking at a company in total. 'Between 80 and 90 per cent of quality programmes fail because they don't take a holistic approach,' he says. Many organizations concentrate on customers, but if they don't get the infrastructure and culture right, their programmes will not work: it is particularly important that a system enables staff to make decisions that will help the business run more smoothly. For example, Rank Xerox has given employees handling customer complaints the power to settle claims up to a value of £200. The idea is that the waste of management time resulting from referring such matters upwards would cost much more – and, at the same time, by delaying a decision, could frustrate and annoy the dissatisfied customer even more.

Further, Rank Xerox has put its money where its mouth is, so far as rewarding customer satisfaction is concerned. Every month 10,000 customers receive satisfaction-feedback questionnaires, and the responses have a direct impact on the pay-packet of the employees. Bonuses related to customer satisfaction account for 30 per cent of executives' income and 3.5 per cent for all other staff. Moreover, managers are constantly appraised by senior staff and subordinates. Failure to be seen as a 'role model' by these significant internal 'customers' is a 'knock-out factor' for anyone seeking promotion. Such practices are seriously life-threatening for the old-style command-and-control managers in Rank Xerox, several of whom have left because they cannot adapt to the new criteria of effectiveness.

Moral: When the going gets tough, the tough get going – but it often takes a desperate situation (imminent corporate collapse) before organizations will adopt desperate solutions (like customer care!)

14. *The Royal Automobile Club (RAC).* Up to 1985 the RAC was, in effect, a gentlemen's club, with an institutionalized and militaristic management structure. When change occurred, the catalyst was Arthur Large, appointed RAC chief executive in 1985. He believed that 'what the motorist wanted most was for his motoring organization to answer the phone quickly, to get to him quickly and to remobilize him.' Among the developments pioneered by Large was that, instead of having a card with 34 different emergency numbers, RAC members could now call a single telephone number. There was enormous investment in IT; aggressive partnership deals with motor manufacturers; and a streamlining of the RAC hierarchy. By 1990, the RAC was able to generate a £7 million profit on a turnover of £155 million, whereas the AA made £4.1 million on a turnover of £231 million.

Moral: Better customer service has to be driven from the top and has to be linked with wider structural and cultural reforms.

CONCLUSION

These stories reveal a mixed bag of success and failure, but already some of the key issues have been identified, together with plausible explanations for scenarios where enormous 'investment' in customer care doesn't generate an adequate return, or any return at all. These issues will be discussed at greater length in subsequent chapters. However, let's finish with yet another anecdote, this time about an unnamed company, specializing in women's clothes and operating hundreds of high street shops.

Recently the organization appointed a management development manager who, though an expert in management development, knew relatively little about retailing. She was told by the managing director that the single emphatic message that was being transmitted everywhere in its shops was the vital importance of positive customer service. It was agreed that the management development manager would work, incognito, as an assistant in one of the shops for a week, in order to get a flavour of what it was like at the sharp end. On her first day, she asked the supervisor what she was expected to do. 'Stand here by the till,' she was told, 'and when customers come towards you clutching a bundle of garments, count the clothes carefully to make sure they haven't got more than they're claiming. Also, when people take items into a fitting cubicle, find a pretext to look through the curtains, by asking whether Madam is all right, so that you can see they aren't stuffing clothes into their bags, or even putting them on underneath their existing clothes.'

Not a single word was spoken about customer service. It was made abundantly clear that, to the staff on the shop floor, the most important criterion of performance was the avoidance of stock losses. Stock losses were what they were punished for; stock losses figured prominently in the vocabulary of head office people; stock losses, moreover, were directly measurable, both by quantity and by money.

When the management development manager returned, once again she asked the managing director about his priorities. 'Customer service is the most important thing,' he declared. 'No, it isn't,' she replied. 'Somewhere between you and the shop assistants, your message is being lost and has been overtaken by talk about stock losses. Not only is customer service getting no attention from your moment–of–truth people, but it's actually getting worse because the behaviour of shop staff makes them look like a particularly nasty and aggressive police force.'

Moral: People do what they perceive is rewarded, they don't do what they're told will be rewarded. In this case, because stock losses were measurable, people could be punished for allowing them to happen; customer service wasn't so easily measurable, and people weren't rewarded for being pleasant, for smiling, or for eye–contact.

2

WHAT IS 'GOOD' CUSTOMER SERVICE?

WE GET THE CUSTOMERS WE DESERVE

If customers are awkward and difficult, if they present continual problems, if they're always complaining, then we have to look for the causes within ourselves. We may argue that we're attracting the wrong sort of customer – if we had 'better' people they wouldn't make so much fuss – but again this will be our fault because our marketing strategies and corporate profile must be appropriate for the specific customers who approach us, and inappropriate for potential customers who don't. After all, a restaurant with customers who are more down-market than it would like has two options:

(1) It can change its decor, its menu and its prices – in other words, rethink its marketing strategy; or
(2) It can accept the situation, and adjust to the customers it has.

ARE CUSTOMERS EVER EXPENDABLE?

'The customer's always right' is good advice, especially when linked to Noël Coward's verse:

> The customer's always right, my boys
> The customer's always right.
> The son-of-a-bitch
> Is probably rich
> So smile with all your might.

On the other hand, there does come a time when individual customers are expendable, because good will and future business have to be balanced against cost. This applies with equal force to internal customers because the effort invested in seeking to win over the hostile manager or department may be excessive, especially if:

1. You remember that your difficult customer won't be there for ever, and could be replaced by someone more co-operative: you may think it preferable to wait until that joyous day beckons. Waiting can be equally productive with some external customers, too, especially where industrial buying is concerned and you're currently dealing with someone who is implacably hostile to you and what you represent.
2. The hostile 'customer' is already isolated and unpopular in your organization, therefore wields negligible influence over your customers elsewhere.
3. Pre-occupation with large-scale victories over hostile 'customers' may divert attention and resources from the vast majority of your other customers, to the point where they feel neglected.

So, when customers are noisily and continually disruptive, it's worth asking some serious questions about the desirability of withdrawing from the relationship. Such questions include:

1. If the present incident, or sequence of incidents, is resolved in a manner acceptable to the customer, is the future relationship likely to be trouble-free?
2. Should tolerance be shown to the customer on the grounds of good business transacted in the past?
3. Are there any special reasons which might explain the customer's unusually intransigent behaviour (for example, personal stress)?
4. Do you realistically want to retain this customer?
5. Will a severance of the relationship with this customer impact adversely on (a) other customers, and (b) your own team, and (c) senior people in your own organization?

6. Is an additional effort appropriate to mollify and make peace with the customer? If so, how can the effort be designed and implemented, and by whom?
7. If satisfying the customer is going to cost money, can the expense be offset in some way? Might it actually cost you more (for example, through penalty clauses) if you don't placate the customer?

Dispensing with customers is not an action to be taken lightly. One of the major factors in service fields like management consultancy, public relations and legal support, is the degree to which the culture of the client organization is compatible with the cultural values of the supplier. In some instances the gap between the two is so wide that it is virtually unbridgeable, and it is preferable for both parties to sever links. From the viewpoint of the supplier this may be highly desirable anyway, if their cultural (and ethical) stance is compromised by an association with specific customers who don't appear to be too scrupulous about how they make money.

THE KEY TO CUSTOMER DELIGHT: THE TRUE MEANING OF 'QUALITY'

Put simply, *quality is what the customer says it is*. This means that any definition of quality generated by the service provider or manufacturer is immediately suspect because it is likely to reflect *internal* criteria (and even wishful thinking) rather than an accurate grasp of marketing reality. Moreover, if quality is what the customer says it is, then the definition of acceptable quality, for any given product or service, may change if customer expectations move on, or if the customers themselves are replaced by different people who have more (or less) sophisticated perceptions.

Some would argue that quality, in more detailed terms, involves:

> **supplying customers with what they want, to
> the standard and specification they want, with
> a predictable (and acceptable) degree of re-
> liability and uniformity, and at a price that
> suits their needs.**

This is fine so far as it goes, but taken literally it implies
that achieving quality is inevitably a reactive and responsive process, rather than proactive and innovative.
There's nothing wrong with being responsive, of
course – God knows, there are plenty of organizations
that don't yet meet even that requirement – although
the result will be customer *satisfaction*, that is, a mental
state of taken-for-granted quality so far as the service
provider or manufacturer is concerned. The danger is
that quality (represented by effective customer service)
comes to be regarded as the norm and therefore ceases
to be noticed. What *is* noticed, however, is behaviour
that violates the accepted and visible customer-service
standard – and so the organization is remembered only
for what it does badly, while what it does well is
ignored.

The same can happen to people within the organization,
especially if they perform services that are invisible so
long as the 'customer' expectations are met. If your
salary slip arrives on the designated day, do you ring up
the administration people to congratulate them? Of
course not, unless you were trying to be deliberately
satirical. If you arrive at your factory one day and discover that it has not burned to the ground, or been van-
dalized, do you seek out Site Security to thank them for
their conscientiousness? Again, the answer is of course
not: you only notice Site Security when there have been
overnight 'incidents'.

Customer delight – for both organizations and internal
service providers – requires activities designed to make

your customers positively and consciously aware of what you're doing for them. And you don't achieve customer delight, by the way, by simply withdrawing your services for a day or two, so that people gradually realize what they are missing. Instead, customer delight presupposes a *constant need to keep at least one step ahead of the customer*:

- Raising standards beyond those currently expected by your customers, so that they are genuinely gratified instead of merely satisfied
- Introducing new forms of customer service in advance of customer expectations, through a process known broadly as service marketing.

I term this whole approach the *Tetley Round Tea-bag Tactic*. Tetleys had already established a powerful market share for their square tea-bags, but went one further with the round tea-bag (claiming, for this premium-priced product, that it offered a rounder flavour). There had been no consumer pressure whatsoever for the introduction of a round tea-bag, so its production was as clear a case of innovative marketing as you're ever likely to meet. Once they met the round tea-bag, however, customers realized what they'd been missing and willingly paid the higher price. So positive customer service should not only mean providing customers with what they want, but also supplying customers with what they want before they even know they want it.

Most customers are easy to please. They simply want us to do what we say we are going to do when we say we are going to do it. When organizations lose customers, they do so because:

- Customers die (1%)
- Customers move away (3%)
- Customers naturally float (4%)

- Customers change on recommendation (5%)
- Customers go because they can buy more cheaply somewhere else (9%)
- Customers are chronic complainers (19%).

But, most of all:

- **Customers go elsewhere because the people they deal with are indifferent to their needs** (68%).

Customers are not just the icing on the cake: they *are* the cake. The icing is an improved reputation and higher profits as a result of a quality job (always as perceived by the customer).

ENCOURAGING CUSTOMERS TO COMPLAIN

You and your customers should be friends: the best improvement ideas are likely to come from them (just as shop-floor workers are the best people to ask when looking for changes in production methods). A wise organization uses information from customers to improve quality and service. Several Japanese firms have been encouraging consumer feedback by including this statement on their product packaging:

'Accepting bad products without complaint is not necessarily a virtue'

Such observations are essential because *most customers don't complain*. Instead, they quietly switch to another product or service, or they stop using the product or service altogether. The latter option is especially popular when the offending product or service is being supplied internally: customers cannot go elsewhere for, say, management training, but they can vote with their feet simply by withdrawing nominees, by slow responses, and by apathetic behaviour.

Yet customers could be persuaded to remain loyal if they felt that complaints were encouraged. Not only that: customers must also believe that if they complain, their complaints will be taken seriously and could conceivably lead to product or service improvements.

You can encourage your customers to help you make/provide a better product/service by asking them to complain. Try these guidelines:

- *Make it easy for people to complain:* Use complaint forms and 0800 (free) phone numbers
- *Ask for complaints:* seek out customers at random and ask them for their views
- *Pretend to be a customer:* contact your organization from outside, as Robert Townsend did when he was president of Avis
- *Listen to the complaints without becoming defensive:* ask questions, ask for suggestions (what can we do to put it right?), ask what you should have done, ask what the customer expected in the light of the behaviour of other organizations
- *Act quickly and with goodwill to solve the problem*
- *Replace defective products immediately or repeat the service* (whichever is the more appropriate)
- *Take positive steps to prevent a recurrence:* don't assume that the first complaint is simply a one-off. Even if it is it's a one-off too many
- *Use some imagination in finding ways to secure feedback.* If you're in the personnel function, for example, you could ring up some of the people who came for interview (and who have been rejected) to ask them how they were treated and if they have any suggestions about how their processing could have been improved
- *Award positive recognition for customer feedback:* small prizes for completed questionnaires drawn out of a hat.

To bring the concepts of quality and customer service closer to home, you can apply the same tests (with a little modification) to your internal customers as well as to your external customers. Think of your internal customers as your personal customers. They can be quickly defined as those colleagues who receive the work that you process or complete.

Arguably your personal customers should be treated even better than your outside customers, because you'll be seeing them again.

THE FOUR FUNDAMENTALS OF CUSTOMER SATISFACTION

Variables related to the product or service itself

Of course, what you actually do for your customer is always going to be a key determinant of customer perception. In discussing this point, the word 'design' is relevant: the design of a product is evident enough, but we can also talk about the 'design' of a service in terms of the way it is packaged, labelled, presented and delivered. Design, for both products and services, is so important that a well-designed product or service will often be capable of surviving despite the most abysmal management of other aspects of the marketing mix. Think about the Jaguar XJ6 of years gone by, for example.

Design features of a product or service affect customer satisfaction in two ways:

- The design sends 'messages' to the customer about the organization's basic values, especially concerning the trade-off between cost and customer. Does it seem that the organization is interested in keeping its customer happy, or in minimizing its costs? Little is more damaging to customer satisfaction than users perceiving that cost savings have been made at their expense: indeed, most customers will gladly pay a premium for a product or service that is just right, and moreover will often see the supplier of the higher-priced item as the one that cares more about its customers.

- Design can enhance or restrict the organization's ability to keep the customer happy during and after the sale. A strong, successful design increases the confidence of front-line staff, while a poor design makes them defensive. Bad design places constraints on promotional messages and also on distribution-channel choices; it can also add considerably to the cost and difficulty of providing customers with adequate after-sales support services.

Nowadays, customers expect systems (for example, workplace technology, procedures for handling planning applications, supermarket layout, mechanisms for paying bills through a bank) to be user-friendly. This means that the *design* of such systems must begin with the convenience, intelligence and sophistication of the people who are going to use the system, rather than the people who built it. Some systems, in fact, give the impression that they have been designed without any concern for people at all, whether customers or employees.

A clear example of an unfriendly system is the application form for insurance aimed at people over 55 years of age, but containing such small print that few people in the target age group would be able to read it without the aid of spectacles.

On the other hand, there are cases where the preferences of the customer and the interests of the organization coincide. One instance concerns the speeding-up of transactions at supermarket check-outs: the use of bar-codes, the automatic printing of transaction details on custom-ers' cheques, and so on. For those waiting in the queue, these innovations are good news.

Variables related to sales and promotion

Three key factors affect customer satisfaction in this area:

- 'Messages' which help to shape customers' ideas about the product or service benefits before they have experienced them in use
- 'Attitudes' of everyone in front-line roles: recep-tionists, telephonists, service engineers, planning officers, check-out operators, bank clerks. These 'attitudes' embrace such elements as:

  (1) Courtesy and helpfulness;
  (2) Level of technical knowledge (and willingness to share it);
  (3) Their approach: are they interested in meeting the needs of the customer or merely in 'selling' them any product or service, however un-suitable, irrelevant or even counter-produc-tive?

- 'Intermediaries' who may be employed to act on behalf of the organization but aren't the organiza-tion's actual employees. Examples include brokers acting on behalf of insurance companies, the use of self-employed 'agents', loss adjusters (who are often seen as representatives of their commission-ing companies), and sales staff for concession units in large department stores. The behaviour of such people offers a rich opportunity for damage to the organizations they claim to represent, a fact that emphasizes the need for stringent recruitment, selection, training and performance-evaluation cri-teria for intermediaries.

Variables related to after-sales

There are two aspects of after-sales that are especially significant for organizations:

- 'Support services' – covering traditional after-sales activities such as warranties, parts and service, and user training;
- 'Feedback and restitution' – the way the organization handles complaints, and the level of priority attached by management to such activities.

In case any reader has doubts, variables connected with after-sales are just as relevant to internal service functions as to the services we may provide for paying (external) customers. For example, it is not enough, when a new procedure has been invented, simply to circulate memos or briefing notes about it in the expectation that every recipient will automatically comply. Some won't have seen the documentation; some will pretend that they didn't see it; a good proportion will misunderstand it, or won't understand it at all (and will therefore throw it in the bin); some will deliberately misunderstand and watch what happens; some automatically reject anything emanating from your office or department; some will understand, see the necessity for what you're introducing, and even feel positively disposed toward you, but have other (higher) priorities or pressures. So what can you do? What *should* you do?

First, the new procedure must be 'sold' and not merely presented as a fait accompli. Selling means that the *features* of the procedure are translated into *benefits* for the recipients: you must show how the new way of doing things is going to benefit them, rather than you. If you can't do this, then you have no hope of persuading your 'customers' to 'buy' your product, other than through threats and sanctions – which will work, after a fashion, but which will generate a number of undesirable by-products and unfortunate side-effects.

Second, the new procedure must be designed with the users and customers in mind. This typically means putting together a first draft of the accompanying manual (or whatever form the documentation will take), then market-testing it on a small sample of actual users. Their feedback will make you painfully aware that they operate on a different wavelength from you, but you have to console yourself with the thought that at least you've learned something from the exercise.

Third, the distribution of information about the procedure has to be accompanied by at least the opportunity for face-to-face instruction (perhaps short training workshops organized on a departmental basis). It's no good simply asking people to contact you if they have problems, because we've already discovered that *the majority of dissatisfied customers never complain.* So you have to get out among the customers – it's called networking – and find out for yourself, by asking the right questions ('What problems are you having' rather than 'Are you having any problems'), listening attentively to the answers, and responding helpfully with clarification and advice.

Fourth, you have to keep up the good work. It's essential to keep a record of the typical mistakes and omissions made by your 'customers' when filling in your forms or complying with your procedures: even a one-off error may tell you something about the ambiguity of your paperwork, for example. Revisions of your 'product', especially when well publicized, will help to persuade your customers that you have their best interests constantly in your mind. What you have to work hard to avoid is the mentality that regards customers as a nuisance and mistakes made by customers as final proof of their extreme mental incapacity.

Variables related to the organizational culture.

The crucial question here is whether the corporate culture is built around maximizing customer satisfaction, or whether management merely pays lip service to it.

- Would an employee postpone a meeting with the managing director in order to deal with a customer first?
- Better still, would the managing director react favourably or otherwise?
- Do staff 'go the extra mile' and overcome all obstacles in order to resolve a customer problem?
- Do the visible symbols of the corporate culture help you to believe that the organization is serious about its customers? Do the signs at the shop entrance, for example, say 'NO DOGS ALLOWED' or do they say 'GUIDE DOGS WELCOME'? It is through such apparently insignificant signals of this kind that the 'culture' of the organization is revealed.

We have to distinguish carefully between the 'formal' and the 'informal' aspects of corporate culture. Formal values are outlined in mission and vision statements, procedures, and other formal control systems. Sometimes, as we've seen already, these formal values operate as little more than a public relations smokescreen behind which the organization actually behaves quite differently. A few years ago, an article in *Management Today*, referring specifically to the International Publishing Corporation, said that the contrast between its published objectives and its actual behaviour was 'nothing less than astounding'.

Formal values will only be meaningful, therefore, if they are supported by the right informal culture. These informal values develop over time, and are shaped by such factors as:

- The extent and manner of senior management involvement
- The degree to which senior management practise leadership by example and act as positive role models for customer service

- The consistency with which customer-care policies are implemented
- The commitment of middle management (who are often the most significant sources of resistance to change)
- The existence of reward systems that genuinely recognize customer service
- The anecdotes and legends that circulate within the organization about past practices, historical events, and current priorities.

It is usually these informal values that determine the true measure of the organization's intentions towards its customers. Organizations seeking to develop, transmit and perpetuate a customer-care culture must ensure that among the new culture's communication gatekeepers (that is, senior management, the chief executive, in-house trainers, external consultants) there is no whiff whatsoever of doubts about the policy, uncertainties about its implementation, and anxiety about its outcomes.

The slightest sign of cynicism will be seized upon by those who would prefer things to remain as they are, and then disseminated widely, with suitable embellishments as the story passes from mouth to mouth. Such stories will be believed (especially by those who want to believe them). They will be viewed as evidence of management's *real* intentions, particularly if there is any historically well-founded justification for thinking that management is capable of speaking with a forked and hypocritical tongue.

It does not matter that a slightly facetious, cynical and throwaway remark made by a communication gatekeeper for the customer-care culture is only a single drop of a sentence compared with the oceans of cogently written and fervently spoken words promoting the opposite message: it will still have precedence.

No amount of denial and disowning will work. Indeed, the very fact that management works hard at distancing itself from expressions of negative sentiment will be construed as further proof of the actual truth.

MAJOR ELEMENTS OF CUSTOMER SATISFACTION IN SERVICE INDUSTRIES

It's become accepted wisdom in service industries that customer satisfaction (and, even better, customer delight) is overwhelmingly influenced by front-line staff courtesy. Many service-enhancement programmes have been aimed specifically at this 'moment of truth' scenario through techniques like behaviour modelling and Transactional Analysis.

Certainly a bad experience at the 'moment of truth' between customer and front-line staff can deter people from buying a product or service. On the other hand, it's worth looking at the results of studies like the ASQC Gallup research in the USA (1985), which generated a database of complaints originating from various service sectors such as car repairs, banking, insurance, the public sector, hospitals, and airlines. The breakdown of major sources of complaint shows the major factors to be (in order of importance):

- Job not done right
- Too slow
- Too expensive
- Indifferent personnel
- Unqualified personnel
- Lack of courtesy.

We have to acknowledge that complaints are not necessarily a good indication of the total spectrum of customer opinion, and also that an American study may not fully reflect customer preferences in the UK. However, the figures are illuminating because they suggest that competitive advantage in, say, car repairs may spring primarily from a correct technical repair rather than from the courtesy of treatment doled out by the staff. As Tom Peters has put it: 'Courtesy does not make up for junk.'

So we have to keep things in proportion. 'Customer care' isn't solely about being nice to the customer, and customer-care training programmes shouldn't become obsessive about smiling, eye-contact and voice control. These things are worth having, but they are noticed more when they are absent than when they are present. In that sense they are like Herzberg's hygiene factors: when provided, they are taken for granted, but when they are missing then the customer will be aggrieved. The customer wants a product or service that works, and no amount of interpersonal competence on the part of front-line staff will deflect him from this objective.

A survey that might ring more bells in the UK was carried out in early 1993 by MORI among a cross-section of almost 1,000 people. According to these re-sults, most of the top five service-provider categories are those with a bedside manner: doctors, chemists, nurses, supermarkets and dentists. At the bottom of the list are public transport, banks, local authorities, motorway services and garages. The results show that 22 per cent of people refuse to use a service again if they are unhappy with the treatment they get, while 16 per cent will try to encourage friends to do the same. But the traditional reluctance to kick up a fuss is still deeply embedded because only 17 per cent of those with a grouse will actually register their complaint.

More than 50 per cent of customers believe that if they are smartly dressed and well spoken they will get good service. One in four feels that the presence of children affects the quality of the service, and 21 per cent imagine a foreign accent to be a handicap.

CONCLUSION: UNDERSTANDING CUSTOMER NEEDS AND EXPECTATIONS

The key to success in customer care lies in full knowledge of the needs, expectations and attitudes of customers. It also relies on the willingness to regard customer care as part of the marketing mix, so that service innovations or higher standards are created, tested and then implemented (or withdrawn) in advance of changes in customer tastes and preferences.

Here are some key issues and pointers based on the arguments advanced in this chapter.

1. **Customer feedback is an essential piece of management information.** The customer who isn't asked his or her opinion may eventually express it by feet-voting. It's no good saying, as some of you readers will be doing, that fortunately your 'customers' are tied to you and so this ultimate sanction doesn't exist. Even if customers can't go elsewhere, they can still decline to take advantage of whatever you are offering, so that eventually you and your function come under critical scrutiny: some or all of you will be made redundant because you are under-utilized. Increasingly, too, 'customers' are allowed to go elsewhere, as market-testing becomes firmly absorbed into the public-sector culture, and as privatization exposes both organizations and their internal activities to the glare of competitive bench-marking.

So customer feedback is indispensable, even if it does seem somewhat far-fetched for prison inmates to be regarded as 'customers' and to be invited to express their views about service improvements to the Home Office. In most service organizations, systematic mechanisms for securing customer feedback can be a remarkably cheap source of market research. Further, the mechanisms themselves can generate useful PR benefits:

customers think they must be important because they have just been asked to complete a questionnaire. Of course, the PR spin-off should be a secondary objective behind creating customer-feedback processes, though in some organizations little attention is paid to questionnaire or interview responses because merely having the feedback process is sufficient in itself.

With some types of organization – hotel chains, tour operators, airlines – questionnaires and interviews about service delivery are part of an established pattern, even if the questionnaires and interview schedules are often badly designed. Other categories of business are getting in on the act – banks and insurance companies, for example – but many are dragging their feet. When were you last asked to assess the service-delivery standards of your nearest hospital, your solicitor, your local authority's planning (or refuse collection) department?

2. **The customer needs and expects 'customer-friendly' systems.** One of the principal reasons for the success of FirstDirect, the 24-hour, seven-day telephone banking system initiated by Midland Bank, is that customers don't have to submit themselves to what they (perhaps guiltily) visualize as critical appraisals from face-to-face encounters with bank staff, nor do they have to enter physically intimidating banking halls. That's on the negative side: on a more positive note, FirstDirect devotes emphatic attention to communication skills among its people so that they answer the phone quickly, in friendly and often Yorkshire tones (which, research claims, people throughout the UK find agreeable). It's worth mentioning that First-Direct keeps on top of its customer standards by undertaking an independent NOP survey each year: the 1993 results show 87 per cent of customers to be 'extremely' or 'very' satisfied. Indeed, FirstDirect claims the highest level of customer service in its field, whilst freely acknowledging that this is not much of an accolade because the competition is so poor.

3. **It's not enough to give good service: customers must *perceive* that they're getting good service.** This reflects the point, already made, that the goal is *not* customer satisfaction, but rather customer delight. Delight occurs when customers receive service that is better or faster than they would have believed possible, when mistakes are openly acknowledged and rectified without argument, and when customers are asked for feedback before they've even thought of complaining. The secret of turning customer service into a competitive advantage is to do something that makes you memorable and therefore different:

- Contacting car purchasers a fortnight after they've taken delivery, to check that the product is meeting their expectations
- Writing personal letters to at least some of your dissatisfied customers, if you're Richard Branson and your company is Virgin Atlantic
- Offering your office, car and home phone numbers to your customers so that they can complain to you (or praise your services) at any time of the day or night, if you're Bob Wiper, chief executive of National Tyres and Autocare.

4. **The customer isn't concerned with and can't be bothered with the problems facing the organization.** Staff shortages, computer breakdowns, power cuts, pressures of work, somebody being out to lunch – all these are managerial problems and shouldn't be offloaded on to the customer. It comes to something when a complaints department, apologizing for taking so long to answer the telephone, defends itself by saying how overworked they are.

5. **Customer loyalty can be built to the level where it is relatively durable, but it is not a factor common to all services.** People are more loyal to their

banks (probably through simple inertia on the grounds that they can't face the headache of transferring all their direct debits) than they are to their dry-cleaners. Virtually nobody is loyal to a petrol company, so strenuous efforts are made to generate a spurious kind of loyalty through 'gift' vouchers and a trading stamp mentality. Even where customer loyalty is relatively strong, it can quickly be destroyed by a failure to meet expectations. The examples often cited in any discussion of customer loyalty are Mark & Spencer and one or two other companies like Sainsburys, but these appear to be exceptions, paradigm cases. They're none the worse for that, of course: many organizations must lie awake at night, dreaming of the day when their reputation with customers is so high that, when they make a mistake, they are actually forgiven!

In fact Marks & Spencer doesn't do anything particularly magical in order to inspire phenomenal levels of customer loyalty. It supplies high-quality (if boring) products at premium prices; the staff are courteous, helpful and knowledgeable (and not just about their own product areas); they exchange goods without question; the shops are clean, bright and attractive. Moreover, Marks & Spencer is not infallible. Some may recall the days when no M & S store had changing rooms where customers (particularly women) could try their prospective purchases: it took an M & S foray into Paris, where customers simply refused to buy unless changing rooms were provided, before the company could be persuaded to be more flexible and correspondingly less arrogant. Another instance of Marks & Spencer insensitivity (to put it no higher) is the British town with two separate M & S stores: until recently, one sold women's lingerie, and the other sold women's hosiery, so female customers requiring both underwear and tights had to traipse from one shop to the other. This may have been some machiavellian plot to force customers to patronize both stores (just as supermarkets make you walk all over the place in order to find the bread), but if so it was remarkably counter-productive.

6. **Intelligent organizations need to find out the precise benefits being sought by their customers.** In any given market segment, customers want different things, and they want them in differing degrees. Here are some of the things your customers *could* expect from you (and these expectations apply with equal force if you're supplying an in-house service to some internal customers, or if your dealings are with people not normally classified as 'customers', like tax-payers):

- Confidentiality
- Cheapness and the absence of frills
- Quality and luxury: the best that money can buy
- Excitement, thrills and adventure
- Attractive, clean and bright surroundings
- Punctuality, speed of service and the absence of queues
- Freedom of choice
- Safety and security
- Status and prestige
- Absence of 'hassle', with no worries and everything taken care of
- Flexibility: the service tailored to meet the needs of individuals
- Friendliness and courtesy, coupled with VIP treatment
- Consistency and reliability.

Systematic methods for finding out customer preferences (rather than a reliance on wet-finger-in-the-air guesswork and 'intuition') are discussed in a later chapter. When you've winkled out your customer priorities, however, and matched them against customer perceptions of how well you're doing for each of the factors involved, you can produce a chart based on the following framework.

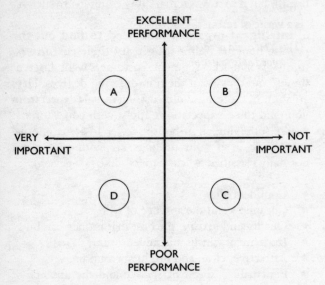

Quadrant A: Keep up the good work
With customer-relevant factors falling into this quadrant, you are supplying high-quality service in elements that your customers regard as important. Concentration on these factors and this standard of service should never flag: indeed, you could profitably devote some resources (though not many – if you have scarce resources there's another quadrant that should receive a bigger slice) to achieve competitive advantage by raising your performance even further. If you're an insurance company, for example, you could speed up the payment of claims from a typical eight working-days, to, say, six days. If you're performing an activity where zero-defect performance standards represent a realistic (albeit challenging) option, you could aim for such standards, not just on special zero-defect days, but all the time.

Quadrant B: Overkill

You're supplying excellent performance in factors that your customers don't regard as all that significant. This is a waste of resources. Sensibly, you have two options:

(1) *You could persuade your customers that whatever you're good at is something that they should regard as important* – in other words, you try to persuade your customers that they've got their priorities wrong. This is very dangerous, and will almost certainly fail: think of the attempts Volvo have made over the years to make drivers think favourably about their all-day lighting system. British purchasers of Volvos took it on the chin, their desire for a Volvo overruling their irritation at being periodically flashed by oncoming cars, but eventually Volvo had to reduce the illumination emitted by the lights in order to make them more acceptable. And French customers, of course, would have none of it in the first place. Another instance, also concerned with the motor industry, concerns the fashion for talking computers (telling you to 'belt up' and the like), eventually withdrawn because drivers did not regard this supposed 'benefit' as a benefit at all.

(2) *The other option is to do what Volvo did eventually, namely, to bow to your customers' preferences.* You won't secure a competitive advantage by offering customers high-quality service in a field about which the customers are indifferent. Indeed, you will lose whatever competitive advantage you have because your scarce resources are being concentrated in the wrong direction, and areas where you should (or could) be profitably raising standards will be starved of time, effort, people and money.

Quadrant C: Low priority

Here are some factors that are not perceived as important by your customers, and where your own service standards are, at best, indifferent. If you increase your efficiency with any of these factors, you will simply move customer perceptions into Quadrant B, and you will be no better off. Actually you will be worse off, because you will find that your improved performance is bringing you no benefit: but if you then try to reduce your performance to its previous level once more, your customers will scream with pain. This phenomenon is a perennial hazard with employee benefits. An organization will introduce, say, free-vend beverage machines in an effort to raise productivity. After a while they discover that productivity has actually fallen because of the time people spend at the machines, queuing for the machines, or asking colleagues whether they want a drink from the machines. So the management tries to alter the system so that drinks now cost a nominal coin-in-the-slot sum. The result, predictably, is a riot of resistance, anger and all-round alienation.

Quadrant D: High priority

This is where your attention must be focused: on activities that your customers perceive as significant but where they also perceive your performance to be poor. Your standards may be poor in absolute terms, or simply poor in comparison with what is being achieved elsewhere. It makes no difference, although if the customer verdict is founded on better experiences elsewhere, then at least you have a benchmark to meet or preferably to exceed.

As with Quadrant B, you have two options:

(1) To do better; or
(2) To persuade your customers that their expectations are unrealistically high.

You have no hope whatsoever of accomplishing (2) if your customers are aware of higher levels of accomplishment being achieved elsewhere. They will argue, not unreasonably, that if one organization can do it properly, then so can you. It is futile for you to assert plaintively that your benchmark competitor, against whom you are being found wanting, is somehow 'different' in certain key respects – he is Japanese, for example, or much larger than you, therefore able to reap economies of scale – because such pleas will invariably be viewed not as reasons but as excuses. It is just possible that you can persuade your customers to reduce their expectations if their standards are founded on an absolute (as opposed to a comparison with known benchmarks), but even so to act in this way is a tacit admission of defeat, a product of negative-thinking complacency, and almost a statement about the indifference with which customers are being treated.

To take a case in point, private citizens have to submit planning applications for alterations and extensions to their private dwellings. Government guidelines apparently recommend that such applications should receive a decision within eight weeks, yet in many instances (it varies between local authorities) definitive replies take longer. If people were asked what might be a reasonable response time, they would in all probability specify something like four to six weeks; in a perfect world the ideal response time might be two to three weeks. For anyone keen to start work on an extension or a room in the attic, delays caused by the processing of planning applications are a huge source of irritation. However, planning authorities apparently make no effort to speed up their activities to meet 'customer' wishes; instead, they take refuge in explanations which rely heavily on adherence to some committee cycle, or on pressure of work, or on scarcity of qualified staff.

The position is exacerbated, of course, by the fact that the planning authority is in a monopolistic position: not only can it take as long as it likes, but it need make no effort to produce customer-friendly literature and forms. *The 'customer' can go nowhere else for an alternative service.* Pressure to improve performance *can* be applied if aggrieved citizens appeal to the elected representatives – but the majority do not (just as most dissatisfied customers never complain!), and the success rate for those who do is problematic at best. The result is that the planning authority devotes some of its admittedly scarce resources to the effort of persuading citizens to adopt more 'reasonable' expectations, in other words, expectations more closely aligned with what the planning authority is prepared to deliver.

7. **When considering the purchase of a service, potential customers have to make judgements on factors other than the quality of the service because, unlike a product, the service does not yet exist.** These other criteria can include:

- Information gained from other users of the service
- Recollections of past experiences with that service provider, or with other providers of the same service, i.e. experiences with a specific firm of estate agents (or stereotypes about estate agents in general)
- Responses to the way the service is 'packaged': quality of the supporting literature, clarity of information about fees/prices, and so forth
- The type of premises from which the service is provided
- The type of people employed to deliver the service.

Where possible, putative customers may try to sample the service before entering into any large-scale commitment. They can sit in on courses run by management-training organizations; they can test the efficiency of a travel agency by securing comparative quotes for, say, a round-the-world holiday with designated stop-

offs; they may ask an estate agent to prepare a sales bro-
chure for their property *before* signing an exclusive deal.

8. **Customers notice when the standard of service
falls below their expectations – but they also
notice when it rises above them.** A small bottle of
champagne in an ice-bucket, with a welcoming note
from the hotel manager, costs very little: but because it
exceeds expectations it can have a disproportionate impact on customer-satisfaction levels, to the point where
it generates a conscious customer delight.

9. **Favourable attitudes to a service supplier can be
destroyed by a single experience of bad service.** In
the USA, the Ford Motor Company's 1986 research
suggested that if people buy a Ford and are pleased with
it, they tell eight others, but if they buy a Ford and
they're displeased, *they tell 22 others* (who in turn tell 22
others, with exaggerated embellishments, and so on).
What's worse, some of the people in this disgruntled
communication chain may be influential gatekeepers,
like management consultants, lecturers, broadcasters,
purchasing managers, and key executives wielding
arbitrary decision powers.

3

WHO ARE YOUR CUSTOMERS?

INTRODUCTION: 'CUSTOMERS' AND 'USERS'

External customers are easy to define, so the textbooks say: they are the eventual users of your product or service outside the organization of which you are a member. In *Fast Track to Quality* (New York: McGraw-Hill, 1992), Roger Tunks defines the external customer as '*the one outside the company who receives the final product or service*'. According to this model, the customer may be a 'government agency, a broker, a retailer, or perhaps the buying public'. Unfortunately there are two difficulties with this approach.

Firstly, Tunks (like many other writers) uses the terms 'customer' and 'user' as if they are interchangeable and synonymous. We disagree with this simplistic stance. For most purposes it is worthwhile, and sometimes it's even essential, to separate the two groups:

- **Customers** or **clients** are people who use our services and pay for them
- **Users** are individuals who are affected by or who affect the product or service that we supply. Users are often people who use the product or service we are offering, but don't pay for it.

The distinction may seem academic, but we'll try to show that for many types of activity it is anything but theoretical. Certainly the people you have to satisfy are the customers in the more rigorous sense of the word described above; in other words, people who pay.

If nobody is paying, there is no work to do

If the paying customer is not happy with the product or service we are providing, then we may not get any repeat business and we may not even be paid for the business we secured in the first place. It goes further because the dissatisfied customer may be sufficiently incensed to tell others about us, and we lose (or never acquire) their business as well.

Secondly, the Tunks use of phrases like 'the company' appears to ignore the possibility that other types of organization have customers. Fortunately, the public sector is becoming increasingly customer-aware and even the prison service is conducting opinion surveys among its 'customers' (who are deemed to be the prison inmates). Charitable and other third-sector organizations could equally well regard themselves as having 'customers' or 'clients' as well, although our definition of a customer/client as a person who uses our services and pays for them would not stand up to the kind of scenario experienced by, say, the Red Cross or Oxfam.

These two subtleties about the definition of 'customer' deserve to be explored further. We also need to explore the implications behind the concept of the *internal* customer.

'CUSTOMERS' AND 'USERS': WHAT'S THE DIFFERENCE AND DOES IT MATTER?

If we stick for the time being to the distinction made on the previous page, then clearly some customers/clients are customers without being users, and some people are users without being customers.

An example or two will bring the argument to life. If we take the toy market, it is clear that until recently children were toy *users* but not toy *customers*. Parents not only did the paying, but also did the choosing: firms like Galt and the Early Learning Centre have thrived very well on this principle, where toys have been purchased because parents believe their children need to develop 'acceptable' patterns of motivation. Nowadays the situation has changed radically. Parents still pay, so in that sense they are still customers, but they no longer do most of the choosing. Television advertising, skilful marketing, video technology and parental permissiveness have combined to place most of the toy purchasing decisions in the hands of children. Children have become customers as well as users. Many traditional toy manufacturers have gone out of business because they failed to notice this change in the customer/user relationship. It's worth noting, incidentally, that some parents have become users when they buy video games or model train sets ostensibly for their offspring but actually monopolize these 'toys' themselves.

Another scenario in which customers and users are different people concerns the purchase of corporate vehicle fleets. The principal customer is the organization's fleet manager, whose purchasing criteria may well include such factors as economy, reliability, durability and corporate image. These elements may well prompt the fleet manager to be favourably disposed towards diesel-powered cars, for instance. Quite commonly, sales representatives and managers are markedly less enthusiastic about diesel engines, but their preferences (they are only *users*, remember) may count for little.

One final instance of the user/customer distinction involves training courses. Participants attending courses must be classified as users, since them seldom pay for the course out of their own resources; the customers are, more properly, nominating managers or personnel departments. So, if you are leading, say, an in–company workshop on time management, who should you be trying to satisfy: the users or the customers? The best answer is that the trainer should seek to please both groups, but it's certainly possible to please the users without pleasing the customers, and vice versa, especially as they each may have differing objectives. The customers (nominating managers) want their subordinates to their time better, but the users may think that they are already competent in this field and simply want to be entertained for a day or so. It's certainly not unusual for course evaluation instruments, like feedback question-naires, to concentrate more or less exclusively on the happiness of the users (not for nothing are such questionnaires sometimes known as 'happiness sheets') when, viewed from a corporate standpoint, the satis-faction of the customers is much more important.

The separation between 'customers' and 'users' is well understood by those who have to sell products and services to organizations. It is reflected in the concept of the Decision-Making Unit (DMU), which describes the person or people who actually take the purchasing decision.

Often the DMU will not include any users, the DMU will not be a user, and the DMU will not have consulted any potential users before the purchasing decision is made.

The DMU, whether an individual or group of indivi-duals, will exhibit personal idiosyncrasies and will be subject to social influences and organizational/political/environmental pressures. Within this system, the views of users may exert only a small degree of power; indeed, it may be argued that since the end-users are not buying the product or service out of their resources, but will benefit from the product or service, they have no right to express an opinion on, say, whether diesel-powered vehicles should be the basis of the company car fleet.

Certainly life is simpler if the customers just give the users what the customers know will be good for them. And we can understand why customers might think like this, given that they too have customers inside the organization – typically managers more senior than themselves – whom they are trying to please. These customers are, sensibly enough, thought to be more important than the users who can be relatively junior personnel with minimal influence, power and authority.

Life is simpler when the interests of 'users' are ignored or under-valued – *until it's time to put the product or service into use*. It is then the *users* who will make or break the situation, not the customers. For instance, studies of software tools indicate that 70 per cent of tools that are purchased are never used. Moreover, of those tools that *are* used, 90 per cent are used by just one person or a small group, even when purchased for a large organiza- tion.

This waste of money starts when requirements for a product or service are drafted by a group that excludes the targeted users. Not only does the resulting product or service fail to meet requirements, but the potential users feel no involvement in the process, have no sense of ownership for the product or service on offer, and therefore feel no commitment to give it a fair trial. If anything, they are actively searching for faults, defects, errors, dysfunctions. Think of all the Christmas pre- sents that are never removed from their boxes before being exchanged, because they were bought by people to reflect *their* tastes and *their* preferences, rather than the tastes and preferences of the user.

FINDING THE USERS AND THE CUSTOMERS

When trying to locate all users and customers, both actual and potential, we need to beware of what in the USA is called the Railroad Paradox (see Gerald M Weinberg, *Rethinking Systems Analysis & Design*; New York: Dorset House, 1988).

When railways are asked to establish new stops on a

given route, they may 'study the requirements' by sending someone to the station at a designated time to see if someone is waiting for the train. Of course, nobody is there because no stop is scheduled, so the railways turn down the request because there is no demand.

The Railroad Paradox appears everywhere there are products and services. It goes like this:

(1) The product or service is not satisfactory
(2) Because of (1), potential users/customers don't use or buy the product/service
(3) Potential users and customers ask for a better product or service
(4) Because of (2), the request is denied.

So, because the product or service doesn't meet the needs of certain users and customers, they aren't identified as *potential* users and customers for a better product or service, they aren't consulted, and the product or service stays bad – or is removed altogether.

This process can apply to commercially available products and services, which are eventually withdrawn because potential users and customers don't have the opportunity (or don't take the chance even when it is offered, bearing in mind that the majority of dissatisfied customers and users never complain) to offer advice on what needs to be done to make the product or service acceptable. It can also affect the division of in-company facilities: nobody bothers to tell, say, the training department what they're doing wrong, but gradually the training department's customers manoeuvre themselves into a position where they can go elsewhere. What is worse, the training department makes no effort to change, but castigates its erstwhile customers for their lack of faith and loyalty.

Not unusually, the training department will attempt to compel its customers to return to the fold by asking for the application of budgetary sanctions or strict policy guidelines ('Whenever training is needed, the services of the organization's Training Department must be used'). In extreme cases this may simply mean that training stops altogether because customers, frustrated by their inability to use alternative 'suppliers', simply refuse to rely upon a training department that has lost all credibility.

When we're supplying a product or service, it makes sense to identify all our actual and potential customers or users. A possible strategy is to brainstorm a list of them. Sometimes we can identify customers and users by name, but ordinarily it will be good enough to name constituencies or categories. Here is a group of customers and users which emerged from one brainstorming session with the personnel department of a UK pharmaceutical company.

Customers

    The Chief Executive (managing director)
    The Board of Directors

Users

    Line managers at all levels
    Job applicants
    Students seeking vacation employment
    Students seeking post-university employment
    School-children asking for help with projects
    GPs in local medical practices
    Employment offices
    Private employment agencies
    The company's employees
    Disabled and handicapped employees

Disabled and handicapped people generally
Shareholders
Parent company executives (principally from the
    USA)
School-teachers
College lecturers
The Institute of Personnel Management
Parents of young employees and apprentices
Local police
Department of Employment
Retired company employees and their families
Industrial caterers
People living nearby in the local community
Insurance companies
Cleaners and staff from cleaning companies
Security staff
and so on!

The idea that a personnel department has virtually only
one 'customer' (given our definition of 'customer' as
the person who pays) has a lot to commend it, and gives
the personnel function a stronger, coherent focus. Even
today, some personnel practitioners mistakenly believe
that they exist primarily for the benefit of the
employees or the workforce.

Of course, producing a list of customers and users is
only the start. Bear in mind that this list should not only
incorporate the customers and users you have at the
moment, but also those to whom you might target
your product or service but who, so far, may be unaware of your existence. So generating a list of actual
and potential customers and users may itself enable us to
think of some highly innovative changes to what we
currently do and what we currently offer. Just consider,
for example, how many previously unimagined things
you could do if you headed a personnel function and
realized that your user-constituencies included 'people

living nearby' or 'retired company employees and their families' (assuming that up to now you had established no contact with these groups).

Merely listing customers and users can help to raise consciousness. If you generate a list with 100 names on it (whether individuals or categories), it is axiomatic that no product or service provider can optimally satisfy 100 different user/customer constituencies. What are we to do?

(1) **Some of the constituencies overlap.**
Satisfying one customer or user may automatically mean that we satisfy others, at least to some extent. If we do something to meet the requirements of graduates seeking post-university employment, this will go down well with the Institute of Personnel Management, the Department of Employment, and even, conceivably, with our chief executive who has strong links with several universities.

(2) **The categories are not independent with respect to the resource choices we have to make.**
If resources are limited (as they invariably are), we cannot do everything – which is not the same as saying that nothing can be done. We have to recognize the force of the old maxim, 'There is no such thing as a free lunch,' and trade off one constituency against another. One way to proceed is to apply a conscious user/customer *inclusion strategy*.

Having listed all actual and potential customers and users, we can assign to each customer/user constituency one of three values (F, I or U), according to the way we propose to treat them:

F = Be very Friendly to them
I = Ignore them
U = Be very Unfriendly to them

We should then be able to apportion priorities and make resource-allocation judgements. To continue the example of the personnel department, it may sensibly choose to be very Friendly to its principal customers, and perhaps equally Friendly towards job applicants, line managers and the Department of Employment. It may decide to Ignore groups like school-children needing help with projects, students seeking vacation employment, and shareholders. (Please don't interpret these possibilities as a reflection of this writer's views: the material being produced here is entirely hypothetical.)

The user/customer inclusion process can also focus our attention on otherwise acceptable people for whom we would want to make our product or service Unfriendly. From the list of customers and users for a personnel function, we could single out private employment agencies and school-teachers/college lecturers, on the grounds that typically these people get in the way of what we're trying to do in order to satisfy more significant customers and users.

We often hear of 'user-friendly' products and services, but there may be customer or user groups whom we justifiably want to approach in an Unfriendly way. For example, we want to make the tops of prescription bottles difficult for children to open; we want to protect medical records, personnel records and credit files against inappropriate users. For some situations, we may even want to make the very *existence* of the product or service unknown to certain customer or user categories. This is certainly true of security systems, which work best when potential penetrators are unaware of them. It's also true of some professional systems, like locksmiths' tools and electronic devices for neutralizing car-security mechanisms. There are bound to be products and services that you and I don't know about either, because we ourselves have been labelled as people who should not be treated in a 'user-friendly' fashion.

SOME CUSTOMERS AND USERS ARE MORE EQUAL THAN OTHERS

We can see that not all customers and users are created equal. Not all customers and users are affected by the product or service in the same way; some will buy for reasons that are radically different from the reasons selected by others. It follows, therefore, that feedback about a product or service will reflect these differing values, preferences, expectations and priorities. Later in this book we shall explore methods for finding out what your customers and users think about what you're doing for them; for the time being, however, let's look briefly at the process of trying to find out *in advance* what potential customers and users might want.

The first question is: **Who participates?** Ideally, before a product or service is designed or purchased, every known or potential customer and user should participate in what may be termed the product or service design process. For certain things, such as individual information systems or custom-built houses, such exhaustive participation is possible, and even the norm. On the other hand, we still have to be careful that we are getting the views of *users* as well as customers: maybe the customer (the person with the cheque-book, remember) is telling us what the users want or need. He may do his best to portray their wishes accurately and comprehensively, but it's a psychological and physical impossibility for him to do so because he doesn't see the world through the users' eyes. Even if he was once a user himself, but is now a manager, his viewpoint will have altered. He's probably much more interested in money and budgets, whereas users are more interested in whether the product or service is user-friendly and does what it's supposed to do. The longer he's been a manager, too, the more likely it is that his views will be out-of-date.

All of this assumes that the customer is being honest and well intentioned in representing (reflecting) the requirements of the users. In many instances, customers are much more interested in their own priorities and criteria. Saving money in the short-term may be the overriding consideration, to say nothing of 'political' aspects about whatever decision is made. Of course, customers will pretend that their own wishes count for nothing, and that they are selflessly dedicated to doing their best for their clients (in other words, the product or service users). Nobody but the naive will be taken in by these protestations.

For the majority of products or services, exhaustive participation is at best exhausting and at worst impoverishing.

One obvious way to save time and money is to sample the targeted population of customers and users. At one extreme is a scientifically designed sampling procedure. At the other extreme, we just grab whoever happens to be around. Usually, the best course lies somewhere in between, but the most important rules are these:

(1) *Be aware that you are sampling*; and
(2) *Be aware of your sampling method.*

For rule (1), the key phrase to listen for is *'We've talked to everybody.'* Talking to every potential customer or user of a proposed product or service just doesn't happen. The phrase 'We've talked to everybody' can generally be translated as:

'We haven't given any thought to identifying whom we should

*have talked to, but instead we talked to anybody who was
available at the time when we wanted to do some talking.'*

It may even be true that 'We've talked to everybody'
means:

*'We talked to those people whom we thought would tell us
what we wanted to hear and we found excuses for not talking
to anyone else.'*

Even when we 'talk' to (or with) people, we still have to
interpret and make sense of what they're telling us. If
we have an axe to grind (in other words, we believe in
the merits of a proposed product or service), the danger
is that we will listen only to the favourable and positive
comments.

Any sampling method is prone to error, if only of a statistical kind. Such errors are compounded if, unwill-
ingly, some potential customers or users are omitted
from the sample. For example, a group of architects
placed a model of a company's new office building in
the foyer of the present building. They placed questionnaires next to the model, inviting 'everybody' to comment on the new design. But not everybody using the
building approached it through the foyer, so this sampling technique excluded people using the trade/de-
livery/staff entrances; moreover, it didn't take account
of people who never used the current building at all but
would be going to the new offices.

Another common mistake is to use a *surrogate* for some
part of the customer/user population. A surrogate is not
a real customer or user, but a stand-in. Sometimes the
use of surrogates is unavoidable if the potential buyers
cannot be approached directly. Trouble occurs when
the surrogates (often marketing people) forget they are
surrogates, and start to believe they are actually the

customers, and the people conducting the research forget that the surrogates are surrogates as well, and start to believe that what they are hearing is what they will hear from the actual customers and users. That's the beginning of many major marketing mistakes.

In an ideal world, we recommend some form of *broadcasting* technique for capturing potential customers and users for a new product or service. There are well-established principles for test-marketing studies in the commercial sector, so if we concentrate here on the marketing of internal products or services, we can make use of all organizational systems for circulating information: announcements in the company newsletter, notice boards, electronic mail, team briefing sessions, quality groups. We may not get many responses, and some of those we do attract may not be very helpful, but there will be those that contribute powerfully to the improvement of the final product or service and to the avoidance of costly mistakes.

At one company, only one user responded to a request for input about a large purchasing system in the planning stage. It turned out, however, that this user was from the internal audit department, which had been overlooked in the planning. The auditor proceeded to demonstrate that the basic approach assumed for the project was not auditable, and therefore not permissible. As a result, the project was scrapped. The project team was disappointed, but not nearly as disappointed as if the system had been scrapped *after* it was built, at a cost of £2 million.

THE CONCEPT OF THE INTERNAL CUSTOMER
A crucial concept behind Total Quality Management is the extent to which internal activities relate to the final satisfaction (or delight) of the customer. This is the only way we can concentrate our efforts where they really

matter, in supporting customer requirements and needs. We can then streamline or even delete activity elsewhere, among processes that have little added-value from the customer's viewpoint.

For present purposes, a *business process* is 'a mechanism by which inputs are transformed into outputs'. (Tony Bendell, John Kelly, Ted Merry and Fraser Sims: *Quality – Measuring and Monitoring*; London: Century Business, 1992, p.111.) In passing an invoice for payment, there are various stages that need to be gone through. On some occasions this involves up to 350 distinct activities or process steps. These steps, typically, belong to different people, different departments, sometimes different locations and different organizations. Also typically, there is no process owner to champion the service to the customer throughout the organization. It isn't surprising, therefore, that problems arise when there are handovers between one functional responsibility and the next, owing to poor communication, unclear responsibilities, or indifference to the needs of the external customer at the end of the sequence (who is a genuine customer in that he is paying for it all).

Meeting an external customer's expectations will require a series of internal customer/supply transactions. A number of organizational employees, who will eventually contribute to the satisfaction of the external customer, will take something (an order form, a requisition, a component), process it in some way (even just by looking at it to make sure it meets corporate standards), and then pass it on to the next stage in the supplier/customer chain. The internal customer then becomes an internal supplier to the next internal customer. Ultimately, the external customer is served by the last of the internal suppliers (who is especially important, therefore, because of the moment-of-truth face-to-face contact with the external customer).

Looking at organizations in this way creates a revolution in thinking. Seeing your department's contacts as customers or users, rather than as a damned nuisance, is quite a novelty for some people. We are sometimes struck by the short-sightedness of some service functions who give every impression that they regard requests by and visits from their customers as an unpardonable intrusion into the even tenor of their lives. It wouldn't be so bad if opinions of this kind were confined to confidentially cathartic conferences among the service providers in private, but for such attitudes to spill over into relationships with other organizational employees is unforgivable. Even the expression of sentiments like 'We could manage much better if we didn't have these awkward customers ringing up to complain all the time,' doubtless said facetiously by some frustrated customer-service officer, reveals a deep-seated, subconscious hatred of customers which is best eradicated at source.

For some internal functions, identifying the next internal customer is very easy and straightforward: there may be only one customer, and that is the department to which your partially completed product is sent (for instance, from manufacturing to quality control). Some internal service providers, however, have several internal customers (or users), whose demands and expectations may be conflicting. The purchasing department may be under pressure from one of its 'customers' to buy mobile phones for its sales representatives, while another 'customer' wants a particular make of mobile phone (not on the purchasing department's approved-supplier list), and yet a third 'customer' is implacably opposed to mobile phones for any personnel other than managers (who ironically have least need of them). Inevitably, trade-offs have to be made (remember there is no such thing as a free lunch), so some 'customers' end up by being more satisfied than others.

What are the factors that lead to some internal customers getting better service than others?

In reality, the answer is complicated. Hierarchical seniority plays a part, but so does the centrality of the 'customer' in the organization's power structure. In some companies, the marketing function attracts the lion's share of whatever resources are going (space, people, time, money), irrespective of the legitimate claims made by, say, personnel, R & D, or production. In others, manufacturing will claim priority: much depends, in truth, on the background of the people who run the organization. Another factor is the extent to which the 'customer' has built networking links with the internal service provider: the presence of these links may lead to a faster and more responsive service being available.

As in the external world of 'real' customers, much may depend on the likelihood that the internal customer will scream and shout if the expected service is not forth-coming, or isn't perceived as adequate when it is sup-plied. Sometimes internal service providers will attempt to make a genuinely impartial judgement, if they have only limited resources and cannot satisfy everybody's total needs, but this may simply mean that every customer's requirements will be expressed in exaggerated form so that cutbacks can be accommo-dated.

We may all agree that such political manoeuvering and in-fighting is counter-productive, but once it becomes established it is virtually impossible to eradicate it. Every customer plays political games through fear that if he doesn't, then others will continue to do so and he will therefore be disadvantaged. Even if an individual customer consciously and scrupulously avoids political manipulation, it will be assumed by the service pro-vider that he *is* still playing politics, and so perfectly reasonable requirements are scaled down automatically.

The Tetley Tea-Bag Tactic

For some internal service providers in particular – personnel departments, legal sections, management-services units – there may be justifiable scope for *proactive* marketing. In this way they can:

(a) Offer new services to existing 'customers'; and/or
(b) Offer existing services to new internal customers.

Widening of the service provision, especially coupled with a widening of the customer base, can be useful if only for self-preservation purposes, but can be readily justified on the grounds that such entrepreneurial initiatives help to add value. The argument is that new services (like an internal vacancy telephone hotline, set up by the personnel function) will extend the professionalism of the department providing them; in addition, they stimulate customer delight (rather than mere customer satisfaction) because customers are impressed by the dynamic and innovative stance of the provider. The new service, although the need for it has not been articulated by the targeted customers and users, may yet fulfil a definite requirement and, if so, it will become established. After all, the service provider is doing nothing more than simply testing the market for additional services, just as a consumer-goods company will similarly test the market for new products. If the service fails – it attracts no positive responses, or excites hostility – it can be withdrawn and little harm has been done.

Proactive marketing, then, consists of *supplying customers and users with products or services before the customers and users even know they want them*. It may be that the new service can justify itself very easily on any cost-benefit calculation (this would undoubtedly be the case with an internal vacancy hotline), and can be linked positively to organizational strategies (like the optimum use and deployment of human resources).

We call this the Tetley Tea-Bag Tactic because of the analogy with the round tea-bag. As we've seen, customers already familiar with square tea-bags were not marching up and down demanding round ones. There was no organized campaign, there were no pressure groups, the media had not been mobilized. Instead, Tetley's marketing people floated the idea, created some skilful word-play about a more rounded flavour, and the round tea-bag was a success.

If Tetley had waited for customers to start asking for round tea-bags, then the product would never have hit the streets (some would argue that we'd be no worse off). Yet some observers act as if internal service providers should do nothing more than simply respond to customer needs and wants. Once the customers have articulated their requirements, it should be the job of the internal service department to fulfil these requirements as speedily as possible, and to the specified (customer-dictated) standards.

We regard this as a depressing prospect for internal service departments. By *following* customer demand, they have no opportunity for *leading*. They cannot innovate; their services, and their standard of provision, is dictated by customers ill-informed about what might be done and how well it could be done. The most they hope for is that their customers would be satisfied with what they do; the opportunities for manufacturing *delight* would be negligible. Service departments would become introspective and complacent: if they did keep in touch with the outside world, they would not be encouraged to set and achieve 'benchmark' or 'best practice' standards of performance. The service provider couldn't add significant value to the organization, and consequently the organization would have less chance to add value for its end-customers or end-users.

All of the above has been written using language like 'internal service providers' or 'service departments', which may make readers think we're talking only about functions like personnel, purchasing, maintenance, legal, or R & D. Nothing could be further from the truth. In reality we do believe that *every function, section or unit in the organization is a 'service provider'*. So everybody has a customer for whom they supply a service. The concepts and lessons of proactive marketing apply across the board: they're just as applicable to, say, innovation in the production department as they are to change in the personnel management arena. If someone in the supplies office designs a simplified requisition form, without being asked to do so by the people who currently have to complete the old one, then that's proactive marketing.

Why are internal customers important?

Most people can see intuitively some benefit in managing external customer relationships, because external customers have a choice to go elsewhere. Improving internal customer relationships – even perceiving internal departments as 'customers' in the first place – often receives less attention. After all, internal customers may be captive customers. So why might it be productive to spend a lot of resources on improving internal customer relationships?

The simple answer is that *there is a strong correlation between internal co-operation and external customer satisfaction*. (See Roger J. Howe, Dee Gaeddart and Maynard A. Howe: *Quality on Trial*. Maidenhead: McGraw-Hill, 1992.) To put it another way, when the relationship between internal suppliers and customers is less than satisfactory, then the external customer ultimately suffers.

When organizational employees have to concentrate on struggling to get their colleagues to meet their needs or in covering themselves because colleagues don't meet their needs, then nobody is focusing on meeting the requirements and expectations of the ultimate customer.

If customers aren't satisfied, then profits will fall; we shouldn't forget that the rationale for customer care is *not* customer satisfaction, nor even customer delight, but rather profit. Profit and internal service quality can be linked in what Schlesinger and Heskett have called 'the Service Profit Chain'. (See Leonard A Schlesinger and James L. Heskett: 'The service-driven service company'. *Harvard Business Review*, September–October 1991.) Its links are:

- **PROFIT** is closely related to
- **CUSTOMER RETENTION**. Typically it costs five times as much to attract a new customer as it does to sell to an existing customer. In some instances, where the value of the products or service is high, and frequency of purchasing is low (e.g., motor cars), the cost of enticing new customers is 17 times greater. Anyone who can retain customers has a competitive advantage. Customer retention is closely related to
- **CUSTOMER SATISFACTION** – which is determined largely by the *value* that the customer perceives the product or service to impart. Perceived value results from a comparison of service or product quality with price and the other costs of acquiring the service or product package – in other words

- **EXTERNAL SERVICE QUALITY** – which is likely to be greater in organizations characterized by
- **EMPLOYEE RETENTION** – itself associated

with careful selection of staff, effective training, latitude to solve customer problems, and compensation related (at least in part) to performance. Employee retention stems from

- **EMPLOYEE SATISFACTION** – which is plausibly higher when
- **INTERNAL SERVICE QUALITY** is high.

A focus on internal service quality, therefore, will generate employee satisfaction. Satisfied employees are more likely to stay with the organization, and this continuity breeds sustained levels of external service quality. An organization that is perceived to offer high (and continued) quality will raise customer-satisfaction levels: satisfied customers will come back for more, and will also tell others about the treatment they receive. More customers, and customers who come back more often, mean higher profits.

Who are the 'customers' in the public sector?

A long way back, at the beginning of this chapter, we quoted the Tunks definition of the external customer as 'the one outside the company who receives the final product or service'. We disagreed with this standpoint for two reasons: first, it didn't adequately distinguish between 'customers' (who pay) and 'users' (who don't); second, it seems to ignore the possibility that types of organization other than 'companies' might also have customers.

With some public-sector groups, specifying the customer-base does not present any great difficulty. The Inland Revenue's 'customer' has to be the Government; tax-payers are 'users' in the sense that although they pay tax, they don't pay fees exclusively to the Inland Revenue to meet the costs of the services it supplies. This is not to say that the 'users' are of no account. On the contrary, if sufficient numbers of 'users' of the

Inland Revenue were to become disaffected, or when a particularly vociferous 'user' expresses strong dissatisfaction about the way it is being treated, then pressure can be applied to the Government through political representatives.

It has become fashionable to regard prison inmates as 'customers' of the Prison Service, and to invite them to complete feedback questionnaires about the quality of service they receive. There is nothing wrong with this, although in our judgement there are other people and groups who might more legitimately be described as the 'customers' of the Prison Service: the inmates are surely 'users' because they do not pay to be there. Again, classifying inmates as 'users' rather than 'customers' is not intended to signify that their wishes should be ignored. There is plenty of evidence that if prisoners are unhappy, they are capable of taking individual or collective action to publicize their grievances. It might appear at first sight that such action harms the image of the Prison Service, and relationships with its 'customers' (such as the Home Office, the Government, and the tax-paying public at large who want to feel secure about the incarceration of those who may wish to do them harm). However, a more cynical interpreter could conclude that rooftop demonstrations are a useful means of extracting additional resources from reluctant 'customers', and therefore have their attractions.

One point often made about public-sector organizations – especially so far as local authorities and river or water bodies are concerned – is that their 'customers' and 'users' are very diverse and their interests seldom coincide. People who pay a river authority for fishing rights don't have the same preferences as industrial companies wishing to offload effluent into the same waterway, for example. This simply means that, as with the private sector, public-sector groups have to manage by compromise and trade-off – which probably means that they end by satisfying no one. The issue is surely no different from that faced by any organization which has a multiplicity of stakeholders whose wishes point in every conceivable direction, but whose priorities have to be juggled according to the political weight of any given stakeholder, the extent of mass support for the stakeholder, the funds available, and the ideological preferences of the organization.

With third-sector bodies like the Red Cross and Oxfam, we concede that our definition of 'customer', as a person who uses the services of the organization and pays for them, becomes more difficult to sustain. Perhaps this is why such organizations prefer to use the term 'client' rather than 'customer'. In the charitable field, the person who pays is definitely not a 'customer' of the receiving charity (he may become one in the future), although most sensible charities understand very well the need to keep their donors happy.

They do this by keeping donors informed about the proportion of revenues allocated to the purpose for which the charity has been created, by expressing (and signifying) gratitude for contributions, and by involving donors in the contribution-management process. 'Users' are the recipients of the charitable organization's largesse and satisfying the users is held to be the charity's principal *raison d'être*. As in many other organizations, it is through the satisfaction of the 'users' (sometimes simply the survival of the 'users' if we think of counter-starvation campaigns in Africa) that the delight of the donors is guaranteed. Very often, in such instances, the satisfaction level of the 'users' is not measured systematically through such conventional devices as attitude surveys and questionnaires, because the methods are inappropriate to the situation; sometimes they're entirely impractical, when the charity is catering for the interests of animals.

—————————— 4 ——————————

HOW WELL DO YOU MEET THE NEEDS OF YOUR CUSTOMERS?

INTRODUCTION

Many organizations haven't a clue about how their customers perceive the goods and services they supply. Their attitude seems to be that so long as people 'buy', then the product must be acceptable. This is dangerous nonsense.

First, customers may buy a given product or service simply because there is no option, and they would prefer to purchase what you're offering than to go without altogether. Remember Xerox plain paper copiers: organizations rented them only until something better (Canon) turned up.

Secondly, the fact that a product or service may be 'acceptable' does not mean that it will continue to sell. Competitors may see opportunities; customer expectations may change; customer tastes may move on. If standards don't rise, and products or services evolve, then downward sales or utilization curves will appear.

Worse is the situation where organizations haven't a clue about their customers' perceptions, *but think they have*. In these circumstances there will be no customer surveys, or indeed no investigation of any kind into customer attitudes, because it is widely accepted that the answers are 'known' already.

Another possibility concerns organizations that don't have a clue about their customers' perceptions, and *don't care either*. The organization may believe it is in a monopoly position and its customers cannot go elsewhere even if they wanted to (examples include welfare benefit offices and internal service departments in some companies). In some instances, the organization may take the view that it knows best what customers should want, and will therefore supply them with a centrally designed product or service. If the resultant product or service has defects (it does some things that the customer doesn't want or doesn't do things that the customer would like, or does things inefficiently and incompetently), then this is perceived to be a problem for the customer and his 'inappropriate' expectations.

Some organizations solicit customer feedback or get it anyway, whether they like it or not, and then *do nothing about it*. Hotel chains leave guest questionnaires in every bedroom, but pay no attention to the returns (perhaps because the whole exercise was initiated as a cynical piece of PR manipulation designed to impress hotel-customers with the [false] belief that customer opinions were taken seriously). Such organizations have absorbed only a small part of the message about customer care: they think that collecting data is an end in itself.

Finally, organizations may seek customer feedback and then *reject all judgements that conflict with what they already believe*. This is called cognitive dissonance: the reluctance to accept sentiments or knowledge contradicting our already established information. Reactions to dissonant data include managerial defensiveness, excuses, castigation of customers, aggression towards those who dare to express the forbidden feedback, and an attack on the representativeness of the data in the first place. It is interesting that nobody ever attacks the adequacy of the research design when the results are favourable to the organization.

WHY IT'S IMPORTANT TO FIND OUT WHAT CUSTOMERS THINK

Customer feedback is an essential piece of management information. For service organizations in particular, and internal service departments within organizations, customer feedback can be a remarkably cheap source of market research. You need to be able to find out:

- Who are your customers?
- When are they likely to be your customers?
- Why are they your customers (and not somebody else's)?
- What do your customers want?
- How do your customers feel?
- What do your customers think?
- How can you make your customers feel valued?
- What sort of initiatives would your customers appreciate?
- What can you do to keep your customers?
- How can you give yourself a competitive advantage so far as your customers are concerned?

You may not need answers to all these questions all the time, but every so often you must ask each of the questions in turn (though not necessarily by using the phrases listed here).

If you don't take the trouble to find out anything definite about the psychology of your customers, either because it's not important to you or because you think you know the answers already, you may (and probably will) find that you're taken by surprise when your customers gradually or rapidly go elsewhere.

- If you don't know why it's happening, you won't know where to concentrate your emergency action
- If you think you know why it's happening, but you're wrong, then your emergency action will be misguided at best
- Either way, you won't be in a very good position to apply correctives.

Securing systematic customer feedback is also important because it invariably generates some surprises.

A Swedish study has found that only 17 per cent of customer problems were concerned with whether the product or service worked as claimed. The majority of complaints reflected concern for what may have appeared to be peripheral issues, like delivery arrangements and packaging.

- Procter & Gamble achieved similar results when they opened a telephone line on which consumers could express opinions about P& G products. They received thousands of calls each month, but only about 20 per cent wanted to talk about the taste of toothpaste or the whiteness produced by washing-powder; instead, four-fifths of the calls focused on non-central issues like carton shapes, handle-design, opening mechanisms, print colours, type-faces, and so forth.

Perhaps this scenario arises because when customers are asked if they have any complaints, they want to please the questioner by trying to find something to complain about. This may be particularly true in Britain, where there is a long tradition of complaining, if only in a subdued, introspective and peevish fashion. Because the service provider or manufacturer has concentrated his efforts on the central aspects of the product or service, these features may present little opportunity for the expression of grievances (real or fabricated). So, out of a desire to please rather than because of any genuine dissatisfaction, customers will say something critical about the packaging, the design, the corporate logo and so forth. The moral is: it's necessary not only to secure customer feedback, but also to find ways of evaluating the significance of specific customer evaluations in the eyes of the customer – otherwise we may end up by giving too much weight to throwaway remarks.

Why is measuring 'customer satisfaction' such a problem?
1. **Over-reliance on anecdotal evidence.** Most organizations are victims of the occasional horror story

of a customer transaction that went wrong from start to finish. Such stories are always bad news for the organization, no matter how unrepresentative they are: the tale itself is widely circulated, its very horrific qualities lending glamour to the teller, and every time the tale is told the organization's name is inextricably linked to it, with incalculable damage to reputation, image, sales and even corporate survival. Usually, the problem is not so much that organizations under-react to spectacularly hostile feedback related to a single incident; more commonly, the trap is to *over*-react (with smug complacency) to highly favourable customer comments, based on a one-off experience. A single letter of commendation may be pinned on the notice-board and even used to justify negative responses to large numbers of customer complaints.

2. **Over-reliance on feedback from complaining customers.** Nobody is arguing that complaints should be ignored or denigrated. On the other hand, the problems of those customers who complain may be atypical, and they need to be counter-balanced by the views of those customers who don't complain. Indeed, we need to find out why some people aren't complaining, instead of congratulating ourselves on the fact that we get so few.

3. **Over-reliance on 'customer complaints' as a measure of customer satisfaction.** Many badly treated customers will not complain (not to you, anyway). If they have a choice, they will go elsewhere. If they don't have a choice, they will become disaffected, will use the service as little as possible, and will be hyper-critical of it when they do (though, again, not necessarily to you). They will await the chance to register their feelings, even if it takes many years. Even when given the formal opportunity to complain, dissatisfied customers may decline to exercise their choice

because they have no confidence that anything will change.

4. **Over-reliance on the opinions of small numbers of highly articulate customers, especially those of high status.** If such customers are personally known to the top management, or have media exposure (such as Esther Rantzen), then this process is exaggerated even further.

5. **Over-reliance on outdated preconceptions about the organization's customer-service effectiveness.** As already discussed, this can mean that even when customer satisfaction is being measured by more or less acceptable methodologies, nobody regards the results (if critical) as meaningful.

6. **Over-reliance on complaint filtering systems.** Customers' perceptions about an organization are often based on their experiences with front-line staff. These members of staff represent the organization in the eyes of the customer, and any complaints that customers make are normally directed at this level in the first instance. It takes a serious incident before the complaint will escalate beyond front-line staff. Consequently, it is often difficult for senior management to gain a true understanding of customers' concerns, since they may have little direct interface with customers. This situation is exacerbated if (as is highly likely) the incidence of customer complaints is withheld from senior management: it is quite common, indeed it's an almost universal practice, for bad news to be filtered and diluted as it passes upwards through the hierarchy. Partly this is a defence mechanism for the front-line staff who have to deal with complaints, and might be thought to be responsible for them being made in the first place; partly it

stems from the need to avoid generating cognitive dissonance among senior personnel who are highly committed to the organization and who cannot bring themselves to believe that things are as bad as the complaints suggest.

7. **Over-reliance on the organization's own views about what its customers should think.** As an example, the author recently stayed in an hotel which supplied its guests with a feedback questionnaire asking questions about (among other things) the restaurant. The questions about the restaurant were confined to issues concerned with the food, the drink, and the quality of the service. There was not space for expressing opinions about anything else; yet in the author's judgement it was other features of the restaurant that made him never want to eat there again. These included the inappropriate and excessively loud background music, coupled with the tasteless decor and unprepossessing ambience. The hotel was not interested in what its customers thought about these things, or perhaps believed (even more arrogantly) that its customers had no right to express opinions about them.

How can we overcome the measuring problems?
Given that any technique for gathering information is likely to have some margin of error associated with it, we suggest that a combination of methods is preferable. Formal customer research (surveys, questionnaires) may produce skewed statistics because you are entirely dependent on the customers who return completed forms – and they may well be unrepresentative. Informal data collection (customer-feedback phone lines, short-term front-line experience for senior personnel) encourages an anecdotal culture, which is equally misleading.

It's salutary to recognize that in the UK several forms of

measuring customer satisfaction are not as prevalent as in Japan. A recent survey by the Digital Equipment Company (cited in Sarah Cook: *Customer Care*; London: Kogan Page, 1992, pp. 52-53) contrasted experiences and attitudes in this country and in Japan, by asking the question, 'To measure customer satisfaction, which of the following methods does your company use?'

Table 1: Measuring Customer Satisfaction		
Respondents replying (%)		
	Japan	UK
Personal visits by management	99	91
Personal visits by sales people	99	98
Analysis of complaints received	98	86
Questionnaires	98	68
Observation & assessment by independent professionals	99	64
Focus meetings with groups of customers	99	62
Toll-free telephones	99	27

Customer-service surveys
Depending on the scale and formality of the survey, it may be necessary to secure the demonstrable commitment of top management to the exercise. This is vital if the survey is to involve external customers, and it's nearly vital if internal customers are involved. Monitoring customer satisfaction is a pointless activity unless management have a sense of ownership for the process and are prepared to act on the results.

The *objectives of the survey* have to be defined before the programme begins, together with a budget and a timetable. It's a very good idea to apply the major disciplines of project management to the survey process, with intermediate milestones covering stages like the survey design, questionnaire pilot-testing, collection of results, analysis, report-writing, presentation to management, and implementation of change.

Among the objectives of the survey will be a *precise statement of the specific customer group(s)* to be addressed. Different types of customer have different requirements and different expectations: some may want reliability of delivery on a regular hourly basis (to support Just-In-Time manufacturing processes); some ask for an unusual range of financial options; others hanker after the highest possible standards of after-sales support. The needs, expectation and satisfaction levels may fluctuate greatly between corporate and tourist passengers of an airline, for example. It may be possible to classify customers by type (as airlines often do, in fact); alternatively we may consider the service we give by market segment, geographical area, size of account, or some other relevant variable. The research may show that there are differences in customer expectation which we can exploit by offering different levels of service to match the needs of particular sectors, possibly withdrawing from others or increasing our charges/prices to an economical level. This is exactly what the Forte Hotel group has done by segmenting its hotels into Travelodge/Post-House/Crest/Heritage/Grand groups.

With some customers it is possible that the standards required are higher than we can economically offer. For others, we may be wasting resources by doing more than is needed: our service may be better than some customers or sectors want, and as a result we are pouring water into the sand. If policy-holders with an insurance company expect household-damage claims to be met within five working days, there may be little benefit in reducing the period to three days, especially as this may involve inordinate effort; it may be more worthwhile to target our resources towards, say, more customer-friendly policy documents.

The leader and members of the customer-survey team should be chosen with great care. If you don't have anyone skilled in the design of surveys and questionnaires, someone must be chosen who is able and willing to fund and use professional advice. The customer-service survey leader must also be articulate, acceptable to a wide range of people, methodical and intelligent. Don't forget that information thrown up by such surveys may be unpleasant reading for some people: the survey leader must act as if (and the survey report must be written as if) there is no vindictiveness involved. For this and other political reasons, the survey leader shouldn't be someone with strong departmental loyalties or long experience in one segment of the organization.

In an effort to smooth the path for the survey, and increase acceptance for its results, *everyone concerned should be made aware of the survey's intentions.* Some genuine consultation (as opposed to the mere communication of facts) is desirable, using face-to-face approaches, individually or through groups, depending on numbers and any laid-down procedures for staff participation. Explain the objectives, obtain comment and feedback about the objectives, and modify the objectives if necessary; however, don't allow discussion at this stage on the survey's actual subject matter.

Before embarking on the survey itself, it is useful to *review relevant existing information or research data concerning customers and customer satisfaction.* Typical questions to ask are:

- What do we know about our existing customers?
- What do we know about their expectations?
- How well are we meeting those expectations?
- What will happen in the future to customer requirements?
- How do we compare with our competitors?

- How is the market likely to change in the next three years?

Analysis of your customer groups may suggest that they fall into categories with differing service expectations, so you have to decide which customer cohorts to investigate, whether you can cover all of them, or whether you need to select a random or structured sample. In the case of a very small group of customers, a structured interview may be preferable to written questionnaires.

In designing a *pilot version of the questionnaire* (or interview schedule) it's worth consulting a few customers in order to elicit suggestions about what questions to ask, what topics to cover, and so forth. Service standards should be monitored against what the *customer* perceives to be important, not on what the organization thinks. Maybe, too, the criteria applied by customers are not the same as those applicable to *users*, and you may have to find mechanisms for getting at both target groups. Many organizations concentrate their efforts on what they see to be 'risk points' in terms of customer service (like response times to policyholder claims), and it's important to check that these are also the critical features from the customer's viewpoint. A useful starter is to ask three basic questions:

- What standard of service do we currently provide for our customers?
- Does this service meet customer expectations?
- If not, why not?

A book of this length cannot give detailed guidance on questionnaire coverage and scope, but some likely themes for inclusion are:

- Which of our products/services do you buy/use?

- How long have you been our customer?
- Do we supply sufficient and timely information?
- Is our paper-work well designed, useful, relevant, appropriate and convenient?
- How quickly do we deliver, and is this fast enough?
- How often and by how much do we fail on delivery promises?
- How accurate is our work?
- What is the standard of our customer contact (face-to-face, letter/memo, telephone, fax, electronic mail, newsletters, brochures)?
- When we get complaints, do we handle them quickly, fairly, efficiently?
- What standard of after-sales service do we achieve?
- Do we readily offer advice and support?
- What is our response time to requests for assistance and advice, and is it acceptable?
- What else could we provide for you that you would regard as useful?
- How do we match up against the standard of service provided to you by other organizations (either in the same field as ourselves, or in other fields altogether)?
- Do you know of anything in the customer-service arena that other organizations do for you that either we don't do at all, or don't do as well as they do?

When the draft questionnaire (or interview schedule) has been put together, it *must* be pilot-tested, first within the organization (which may iron out some of the more embarrassing ambiguities), and secondly with a very small group of the targeted customer population. Whether the questionnaire is intended for self-completion (for instance, left in hotel rooms for guests to fill in if they wish to do so) or for postal distribution (like the 1990 British Gas survey of all its 17 million domestic customers), there are some guidelines:

- A brief opening statement should make the objectives of the survey crystal-clear
- There should be a statement of the potential benefits for the *customer* (not the product/service supplying organization). Remember that customers are selfish people, like all human beings, and will only do something (like complete a questionnaire) if they think there's something in it for them
- The questionnaire must be easy to complete, and should therefore be brief and simple
- Supply questions with 'tick-box' answer options where possible (though with some questions you *must* supply an 'Other [please specify]' alternative, otherwise you may miss crucial opinions
- Leave lots of white space so that the survey form doesn't appear intimidating or oppressive
- Leave space for additional comments – though this doesn't need to be too generous because customers with something to say will generally write a letter to go with the completed questionnaire
- Make return easy, through a Freepost address or conveniently placed posting box
- Personalize the questionnaire by giving the name of the person originating the survey and to whom the form should be returned. The name should be very senior (preferably the managing director or chief executive): not only does this add authority to the exercise, but it also conveys to customers something of the priority attached to customer service
- Respondents should be thanked for their participation, by suitable words and phrases within the questionnaire itself; even more impressive, if the numbers are manageable, is a personalized letter of thanks (easy enough to produce on a word-processor)
- Questions should be sequenced logically, grouped by subject and with general issues presented before specific ones

- Don't ask any difficult questions early in the survey form – keep them (and questions on sensitive issues) until later, when the respondent is already 'hooked'
- Personal customer details are best kept until the end; if you put them at the beginning, the customer may think you're more interested in learning about him than in what he thinks about you
- Questions with closed answers (Yes/No, tick boxes) should appear early in the questionnaire with open questions left until later.
- Scalar questions (to rate service factors on a scale of one to five, for instance) allow comparisons to be made, although respondent interpretation of rating scales is notoriously subjective: what is 'very good' to one person may be only 'quite good' to another;
- The best surveys not only ask questions about product/service elements, but also seek to establish the *importance* of each element to the customer: otherwise you could find yourself running around to improve performance in a dimension where customer satisfaction is low, only to find subsequently that customers didn't think it very significant.

Response rates for questionnaire surveys are typically very poor, and you must use an impressive range of devices to persuade people to reply. This is desirable not just to widen the statistical credibility of your conclusions, but also to prevent your information being swamped by, say, small groups of customers with a particular axe to grind. Some of the points mentioned above – creating eye-appeal for your questionnaire, keeping the questions brief and simple, leaving lots of white space – will all help. So will:

- Continual re-emphasis on the personal attention given to replies by some very senior person in your organization, like the Kwik-Fit form which is signed by Tom Farmer, the MD

- Offering incentives for completion, like entry in a monthly prize draw
- For some organizations, the availability of, say, a £5 voucher to every respondent would be cost-effective, or a free sample of one of the company's new products
- For postal surveys, it doesn't cost much to personalize the questionnaire forms
- With self-completion studies, response rates can be raised markedly if the customer is given the questionnaire form in person by one of the organization's staff (for example, the hotel receptionist) with a face-to-face invitation to complete it; this can be reinforced by a further incentive such as a free drink on your next visit.

When sufficient returns have been generated, *the results of the survey must be analysed*, using appropriate statistical techniques if the sample is large and some of the questions have to be cross-referenced against each other (so that, for example, the *satisfaction level* with a particular product/service feature can be contrasted with its *perceived importance*). The outcome should be some answers to the following questions:

- Who are our customers?
- What customer service do they require?
- What customer service do we give them?
- Where are the significant gaps in performance?
- What could or should we be doing to remove those gaps?
- How does our service stack up against 'best practice', 'excellence', benchmark organizations or our competitors (not only in the UK but in other parts of the world)?
- What can we do to move towards those standards of performance?

In open organizations, *the findings will be disseminated*

widely and will be backed up by face-to-face (individual and group) presentations leading to visible and conspicuous action. The organization is even more open if it distributes copies of its findings to the customers who contributed to the proposals for change. Clearly this may not be practicable for consumer organizations, but does make sense for industrial and commercial suppliers who may have no more than a handful of customers (even if they in turn have thousands of users). If you've committed yourself in advance to the distribution of your results and recommendations among your respondents, then this will:

- Increase the likelihood that your customers give you feedback in the first place
- Increase the likelihood that you will introduce visible and conspicuous changes to your customer service standards and processes. Don't forget that there's no point in introducing changes if nobody notices them, because *customer perception is all there is*
- Increase the likelihood that departments and functions inside your organization will accept the logic of your findings and the changes needed. They will know that they are under the microscope, not only from senior management within your organization but also from customers.

Should nothing improve after the survey has been finished, your customers' opinions of you will inevitably deteriorate. Even if you were doing all right, you can't afford to stand still because your customers won't: and your survey will have whetted their appetites. They may have been satisfied before, but your questionnaire will have made them ask questions themselves, and they will now be looking for more than customer satisfaction: they want customer *delight*!

Tom Peters tells of the time he was interrupted by the

president of a department-store group who said, in effect, 'You've no right to criticize us; *we're no worse than anyone else.*' The fact that you are no worse than any of your competitors is no defence: by resting on this complacency, you expose yourself to innovations from a competitor who suddenly realizes that superior customer service is the route to sustainable competitive advantage, or from entryists who see an opportunity in your sluggish marketplace.

The only major trouble with customer surveys is that they may not be very good at telling you what your customers will want tomorrow, or what potential customers might want that would make them look in your direction. Often customers don't know what they want and therefore cannot express an opinion about it, until something new is put in front of them. Most really exciting product or service innovations don't stem from market research, but originate with some bright spark who has a startlingly new, but often devastatingly simple, idea, which has to be promoted against the opposition and inertia of conventional corporate thinking. Think about Post-It Notes and the Sony Walkman. As Johansson and Nonaka write ('Market research the Japanese way', *Harvard Business Review*, May-June 1987, pp.16-22):

'When Sony researched the market for a lightweight portable cassette player, results showed that consumers wouldn't buy a tape recorder that didn't record. Company chairman Akio Morita decided to introduce the Walkman anyway, and the rest is history. Today it's one of Sony's most successful products.'

Other methods for finding out what customers want
What follows is a mixture of quantitative and qualitative approaches, some innovative, and some that are already in use for certain organizations and certain markets. When looking through these techniques, try not

to react to them purely on an emotional basis ('I like the idea of that' or 'It sounds ridiculous'), but think which techniques might work for you, your products or services, and your organization. Some of the best ways of finding out about customers have been developed by individuals who've simply built on what others have done before.

1. **Telephone surveys.** The customer-services department at Kwik-Fit telephones, at random, 100 customers per month to check on customer satisfaction. Apart from being a useful PR exercise, the method generates more or less instant data which can be used for fine tweaking of customer-service strategies. Further, telephone surveys are very cheap, at least compared with face-to-face interviews. There are snags, of course: customers approached by telephone may be reluctant to give their time and even to give information, believing there is a hidden agenda concerned with enhanced sales (they may have already had similar experiences with double-glazing and kitchen-renewal companies). On the telephone, too, questions have to be simplistic as some people have difficulty in coping with attitude/ opinion scales when they don't have a piece of paper in front of them.

2. **Face-to-face interviews.** Again a major benefit is speed of response, but this time the principal disadvantage is cost. Face-to-face interviews can be longer and less structured; they allow for more subtle questioning, and can be especially beneficial in 'fleshing out' the bald statistical data acquired from formal questionnaires. Looked at the other way round, a small number of face-to-face interviews may be used early in a customer survey as a means of generating issues for a comprehensive questionnaire.

3. **'Mystery shopping'** This research method is often

used in the retail arena, but has also been applied successfully in such sectors as catering, financial services and the automotive industry. In a recent instance known to the author, a solicitor telephoned his company's various branch offices, posing as a potential purchaser of domestic conveyancing, to record the treatment he received from first-line reception and telephonist staff, and also the answers and cost-quotations generated by the legal professionals. The results indicated what his firm perceived as an appalling degree of variation in the way potential customers were treated. The tape-recorded encounters were used as a dramatic justification for significant change.

Generally speaking it isn't advisable to use mystery shopping as the sole measure of the effectiveness of customer service. In the case briefly described above, it was taken for granted that the initial treatment received by potential customers would be a major factor in determining whether or not they would award their domestic conveyancing work to the legal firm in question. There was no strong evidence to justify this belief, other than an intuitive conviction shared by the firm's partners: there had been no systematic surveys of such customers which might have lent support to the argument. Perhaps the politeness and friendliness of front-line telephonists counts for less than the company imagined, and therefore to concentrate on this element would not generate significant business enhancement. After all, if there were widely varying approaches used in the firm's different offices, potential customers would scarcely be aware of such variations because they would phone only a single office – and would assume that the answer and information dispensed there would be repeated from other locations. So the imposition of blanket uniformity would not be helpful, other than in reinforcing a 'best practice' model.

Another difficulty with mystery shopping concerns

hostility from the organization's employees. The mystery shoppers are seen as snoopers, spies or detectives, more interested in catching people doing it wrong than in recognizing them for doing it right. To some extent these perceptions and fears can be managed, by making sure that staff members are not identified in mystery shopping reports, or by dispensing individual rewards to staff who excel themselves. This latter approach was used to great effect in ScotRail when managers visited all parts of the system incognito, but armed with £10 gift vouchers with which they could acknowledge special customer-service expertise.

4. **Suggestion schemes.** This device can work well inside organizations, provided it's properly managed, in order to promote service improvements for internal customers. In some cases it can be applied with equal effectiveness to external customers, especially where there is a long-standing relationship between the organization and its clientele.

5. **'Membership groups' of customers.** In the past, customer/user groups such as consumer unions and telephone users' associations have been created for self-defence reasons, arising from a perceived need to obtain negotiating power over product or service suppliers. Such groups can be attracted and treated as members of the product or service organization, or some form of 'owner club' can be created and sponsored by the product or service supplier. Lego has developed the 'Lego Builders Club'; the Harley-Davidson motorcycle owners' group has more than 100,000 members. As Rosabeth Moss Kanter points out ('Even closer to the customer', *Harvard Business Review*, January-February 1991, pp. 9-10), when customers become members their loyalty to the organization is increased and they provide a rich source of feedback, innovatory ideas, and test sites.

6. **'Freephone'.** This idea was started by companies like Procter and Gamble in the USA and is said to be the most popular means of gaining feedback from customers in North America. In the UK the 'Freephone' concept has been adopted by American Express and Burger King; experience with both organizations suggests that only a small proportion of calls are actually complaining about something. The 'Freephone' option is especially cost-effective: even if only 1 in 100 calls supplies a concrete, practical idea for service improvement then the facility has paid for itself.

7. **Video point.** Building on the talkback opportunities used by Channel 4, a few organizations have experimented with video booths in which customers can record their comments. This system only makes sense where customers may be inactive for part of the time and therefore have little to lose: airport departure terminals are an obvious opportunity. Video points represent a therapeutic vehicle for angry and frustrated people; their anger and frustration may be stimulated even further if they've had to wait to get into the booth; so this technique always has to be supplemented by more analytical information-gathering approaches.

8. **Focus Groups.** First-hand feedback from customers can be secured through focus groups (sometimes known as user panels or customer-service groups). Organizations in the UK applying this technique have included BT, Boots, Nationwide Building Society, Safeway, and several computer companies. The idea is simple enough: customers are invited (usually in groups of up to 20) to express opinions about the sponsor's quality of service, at an informal gathering on the organization's premises or at some other suitable venue. Typical topics to be addressed may include:

• Usage of the organization's products and services

- Use of competitor's products and services
- Customer likes and dislikes
- Areas for improvement
- Ideas for new products and services

The PR benefits for focus groups and their analogues are surely impressive (and have been exploited especially by the BBC in its regional answer-back events), but the PR focus can be counter-productive if consumers believe that the organization is defensive and that the purpose of the process is merely to let customers let off steam, without anything tangible happening as a result. Moreover, the customers attending focus groups can be dramatically unrepresentative, either uncritical adherents to the cause or strident and unappeasable critics.

9. **Third party surveys.** One of the most beneficial lessons to be learned from customer service surveys is not only whether your activities are well received by your customers, but how you compare with the quality of service provided by your competitors. Information along these lines is normally secured via syndicated research, where several organizations in the same industry commission independent surveys of customer satisfaction and share the results, thus allowing direct comparison of service levels to be made.

10. **Role reversal.** Senior management is often remote from customers and it can be salutary for its members to acquire first-hand experience by acting for a while as front-line customer-service personnel. At Kwik-Fit, Tom Farmer and every one of his management team spend one week a year working in one of the Kwik-Fit depots: they fit exhausts, change tyres, and are seen by the staff dealing with customers. For some years, Hyatt Hotels in the USA has organized an 'In Touch Day' when management is put into the field as doormen, front-desk attendants and food servers, the argument

being (especially for the hotel business) that it is the employees in the front line who determine the fate of the company.

This type of involvement – experiencing the difficulties encountered by the service provider, keeping close to the customer – not only generates useful customer feedback (albeit on a purely anecdotal basis, therefore to be supplemented from other more systematic sources). It has three other major benefits:

- It helps avoid procedures and policies that in fact make it more difficult for staff to deliver good service
- Obvious involvement helps strengthen the commitment of management to staff
- It avoids the hypocrisy of managers talking incessantly about quality of service, but not leading by example.

MEASURING CUSTOMER SERVICE: CONCLUSION

If, after all the measuring and the anecdotal evidence, we want seriously to check that progress is being made, then we have to ask three questions:

1. *Have staff noticed what we are saying, and do they really believe we are right?*

Regular communication, attitude and 'climate' surveys are increasingly common tools here; as with customer feedback generally, they are much more reliable than one-off, isolated incidents. Senior management has to be cautious about falling prey to wishful thinking if it takes ringing words of endorsement, encouragement and support from middle management at their face value: what counts is whether front-line staff, in particular, have internalized the messages about customer priority. Would they really believe, with Lee Iacocca, that the nine most important words in a company are 'Satisfy the Customer!' (repeated twice more)?

2. *Has staff behaviour changed?*

Internal measures can reveal much of this information on a quantitative basis, including even some elements of service quality (such as timeliness and accuracy of delivery and response times). Courtesy at the customer interface (the 'moment of truth') is much harder to pin down, but as we've seen in this chapter, it is possible to carry out systematic investigations into service performance through 'mystery shopping' and so forth.

3. *Has the customer noticed?*

A frustration often met here is that the rising expectations of customers, coupled with their elephantine memory for failings, can mean that 'real' improvements in quality or service take a disappointingly long time to register. Some organizations have had to run faster and faster just to maintain equality with past ratings, and those that have publicly vaunted their efforts to improve service have reaped a mixed harvest: higher levels of commendation on the one hand, but at the expense of more complaints on the other.

Whatever the results, the regular feedback of customer surveys to staff, preferably on a locally relevant basis, certainly has more power than management exhortation alone. Further, it signals the value that the organization places on customers, however capricious their views.

As a final cautionary caveat, it's worth repeating the point already made several times in this book (not least in this chapter), namely that measuring customer satisfaction and delight will only tell you more about the thing that, in effect, you should already know. Gary Hamel and C K Pralahad ('Corporate imagination and expeditionary marketing', *Harvard Business Review*, July–August 1991, pp.81–92) argue that there are three kinds of company:

(1) *Those that simply ask customers what they want* and
     end up as perpetual followers. For such organiza-
     tions, risk has been reduced to negligible propor-
     tions: they can, instead, face a future in which there
     is the certainty of competitive failure.

(2) *Those that succeed in pushing customers in directions
     they do not want to go* and end up by going out of
     business when their customers eventually can't
     take any more. More pliable and receptive com-
     petitors will take over.

(3) *Those that lead customers where they want to go before
     customers know it themselves.* Go back a decade or
     two: how many customers were asking for micro-
     wave ovens, cellular telephones, compact–disc
     players, home fax machines? How many custom-
     ers, today, are demanding a world in which tele-
     phone numbers are attached to people rather than
     places? Conventional market research, customer
     surveys and segmentation analysis are unlikely to
     reveal such ideas and opportunities:they will come
     only from a deep insight into the needs, lifestyles
     and aspirations of today's and tomorrow's
     customers, going beyond straightforward 'tick-
     box' answers.

     On ps. 176–177 you will find a sample customer
     quality questionnaire: learn from it, adapt it, and
     use it to assess customer perceptions of your own
     organization, department, product or service.

5

HOW CAN YOU MOTIVATE PEOPLE TO GIVE QUALITY CUSTOMER SERVICE?

WHAT MOTIVATES PEOPLE ANYWAY?

This isn't going to be another boring tract about motivation, describing all the major theories produced over the past 50 years, but conspicuously concealing how any of them can be applied in practice. What we do need to do, however, is to summarize the general messages behind these theories, in so far as they relate to ways of motivating people in a customer-care context.

(1) *The most powerful motivator of all is the individual ego.* There is no quicker way of turning people off than to denigrate what they're doing, what they've done, who they are or where they've come from. If you talk to anyone like this, you are attacking their self-esteem, their central sense of identity, their pride and self-respect. Yet some customers communicate with front-line customer-care staff in exactly this fashion. No wonder that some of these staff, driven beyond endurance by a constant barrage of humiliation, eventually retaliate or resign. Of course, we know they shouldn't retaliate, and we don't want them to resign, so some way has to be found of protecting customer-contact people against constant assaults on their egos.

If all this sounds depressing and negative, another way of looking at it is to say that stroking someone's ego is a highly positive technique for enriching employee performance. *People like their egos to be stroked: they can't get enough.* Unfortunately we're not very good at it in this country: we're much better at criticizing, though not commonly in the direction of the target. We're even better at saying nothing, so that people don't have any idea about whether their work is well regarded or, conversely, is likely to result in summary dismissal.

(2) *People are selfish and self-interested.* They're in it for what they can get. Customers behave like this, so why shouldn't customer-service people?

The first question that everyone asks when it's suggested that they might buy a product, use a service, or respond to some customer-care incentive programme, is:

What's in it for me?

Of course, they don't necessarily ask the question so crudely and as explicitly. Whatever they think, though, it will amount to a calculation of the 'costs' and 'benefits' involved. Moreover, the question 'What's in it for me?' doesn't necessarily imply a blatant and self-centred selfishness without regard for the other human beings involved. Clearly there are some individuals who are nakedly selfish and seem to regard other people (even members of their own family) with indifference. We often think of such people as being emotionally inadequate, socially immature, and psychologically psychopathic.

By contrast, the majority of the human race is **self-interested**, which is a bit different. Self-interest means that most people, most of the time, will act in such a way as to maximize the benefits **for themselves** or minimize the losses **for themselves**. In calculating outcomes, however, they will take account of such elements as:

- The impact of their actions on others
- What others will think of their actions: whether

the response will be approval, contempt or indifference.
- Their own sense of guilt which may be acti-
vated if they take actions contrary to their own
internalized moral beliefs.
- Whether their actions will have a positive or
negative impact on future collaborative relationships.

All theories of motivation rely on the fundamental principle of self-interest. Maslow's hierarchy of needs
assumes that people will seek to satisfy **their** needs, not
principally the needs of others; Herzberg says that **individuals** seek self-actualization, achievement, responsibility, growth and so forth **for themselves**; Expec-
tancy Theory, even more openly individualistic, claims
that people will choose actions which they believe
(sometimes mistakenly) will lead to attainment of their
goals.

Transactional Analysis – a model often used in
customer-service training programmes – relies very
heavily on self-interest as the driving force in employee
(and customer) motivation. The concept of 'stroking'
implies that if we administer positive 'strokes' to others
(eye-contact, smiling, 'How can I help you?'), then
others will intuitively feel the obligation to return these
'strokes'. We cannot expect to *receive* strokes without
being prepared to *give* some, otherwise the relationship
becomes unequal and one-sided.

What this means in a customer-care context is that it is
no good trying to construct appeals for improvement
on the altruistic argument that if you supply effective
customer service, you will make the customer feel
better. This will only work if it can be shown (and it
can) that making the customer feel better will make the
front-line customer-service person feel good as well.

Careful recruitment and selection can ensure that people opting for front-line jobs in organizations are the kind who will derive personal satisfaction from dealing with customers. Nor does it make sense to argue that front-line customer-contact people should behave better because that will increase the organization's profits. For a start, that doesn't apply in public-sector scenarios: but even where it does, the reaction of many staff to a profit-maximizing appeal may well be 'So what?' If their commitment to the specific organization is low (it's just a job) and their share of corporate profit is negligible, then the logic will collapse. In addition, the cause-and-effect linkage between improved customer service and enhanced profit is plausible but too tenuous to have behavioural impact.

(3) *The best kind of motivation is internal commitment*

Narrowly selfish people can be made to work effectively in customer-care positions, provided there is a direct and meaningful reward available to them for acting as if they cared about their customers, even if in fact they don't. A selfish person could be told that they will be given £1 every time they smile and exchange eye-contact with a customer: this may make them smile more often. However, their hearts won't be in it. They'll be responding like Pavlov's dogs to an externally imposed stimulus. Their insincerity will eventually communicate itself to the customers, who will then be turned off even more than they would have been by straightforward contempt and indifference. Further, the selfish customer-service person will come to demand greater incentives as the impact of the £1-a-smile scheme wears off; and because the motivation is superficial, it's likely that our selfish person will produce only the responses for which the incentive is applicable – the rest of his/her behaviour (body language, words, tone of voice, speed of response, preparedness to co-operate) will not be congruent with the supposedly positive signals being transmitted on a spas-modic basis.

Internally committed customer-service staff, by contrast, will behave positively towards customers because they find the process intrinsically rewarding. Their words and body language will be consistent; they are less likely to be perceived as insincere and manip-ulative; they will not need crude '£1-a-smile' incentives to make them effective.

(4) *Money isn't everything*

Talk of 'rewards' and 'incentives' in some of the para-graphs above may have misled a few readers into think-ing that motivation is exclusively about money. In practice there are many rewards and incentives available for front-line customer-service personnel which don't cost anything at all, or whose cost is disproportionately low in relation to the benefits. Trying to motivate customer-service people exclusively by financial means is bound to fail. First, it attracts the wrong type of per-son, whose attitude is instrumental rather than in-ternally driven, and who eventually begins to utter con-ventional phrases like 'How may I help you?' in a patently thoughtless fashion (rather as an acquaintance will greet someone with 'How are you?' while simulta-neously making it clear that they don't want an answer, or won't listen to it if they get one).

Secondly, motivating people through financial incen-tives eventually becomes unbearably expensive. Any given level of bonus will come to be taken for granted; recipients will only respond if given more; and like drugs, it takes an ever-larger dose to produce the desired effect.

(5) *People do what they perceive is rewarded, not what they're told is rewarded*

Constant exhortations from top management about the vital importance of customer service will mean nothing if, at the sharp end, employees believe that their immediate supervisors or managers are actually interested in other things altogether – like avoidance of stock losses. In fact, exhortations won't work at all unless they are reinforced down the hierarchy and sustained by some self-interest benefit.

HOW CAN WE MOTIVATE FOR CUSTOMER SERVICE?

Top management commitment

It may be a cliché that top management support is a vital ingredient for change, but unfortunately it also happens to be true. Customer-care programmes driven by non-line functions, like marketing or personnel, are doomed to failure. Senior line management's preoccupation with what it perceives to be the practical imperatives will inevitably lead to contradiction, confusion and role conflict (think of the struggle between customer service and stock losses). So customer care only works when the top team recognizes it to be a strategic necessity.

Leadership from a customer-service champion

There are virtually no successful examples of an orientation towards customer service that have not been associated with an identifiable 'hero' or 'heroine' like Michael Edwardes, John Egan, Anita Roddick, Tom Farmer or Colin Marshall. These leaders serve two functions:

(1) *They simplify reality* by transmitting a clear, straightforward message throughout the hierarchy and towards the external world;
(2) *They are needed to drive through any significant change of culture and values.* This heady mixture of vision and muscle really does make a difference.

Competition and incentives

Borrowing from the world of sales force incentive programmes, this approach offers tangible rewards (financial or otherwise) for proven competence in service enhancements. The snag is that dispensation of the

rewards is often conditional upon adherence to previously published 'standards'. In other words, the behaviour rewarded is that specified within the
'standards', irrespective of whether the 'standards' are
aligned with what customers want, need or expect.
Two years ago the author stayed at an hotel with
'Dover sole on the bone' as one of the items on the
dinner menu. On asking for the fish to be served off the
bone, the author was treated to the response that this
was impossible because it was not 'the standard', in
other words, it did not conform to centrally-dictated
procedures. So, for competition and incentives to be
effective, the rewards have to go beyond mere adherence to 'standards', but recognize instances where
staff have 'gone the extra mile' to generate customer
delight or turn a complaint (problem) into an opportunity.

Recruitment practices

How relevant are your recruitment criteria and procedures to your customer-service culture? What evidence
is there that better-educated people are invariably more
effective at customer-interface skills? The answer is that
there is no such evidence, yet some organizations act as
if the mere possession of a higher-education diploma
and degree could signify customer-care competence.
Here the example of British Airways is worth repeating. For cabin crew, the search for 'breeding' and 'style'
has been replaced by concern for people who are tempe-
ramentally outward-going and friendly.

Induction

A few years ago, staff tended to be taught the technical
elements of their work and were given a few trite messages about customer service as an after-thought. Indeed, even in jobs where customer-management skills
are crucial (sales representatives are a case in point),
organizations would seek individuals with the appropriate technical background and then attempt to graft

on, as it were, a galaxy of selling and inter-personal skills. More companies now recognize the foolishness of these priorities. It is much more worthwhile to take people who already have an intuitive grasp for dealing with people (a *skill*), and give them the necessary level of technical familiarity (*knowledge*), if only because equipping someone with knowledge is easier, educationally, than training them for skills, especially if they lack the behavioural apparatus (attitudes, personality, motivation) to enable them to perform the skills effectively.

If customer service is put across during induction as a veneer spread over the technical features of the job, then when the going gets hot the veneer will be lifted and forgotten.

Nowadays, many organizations will teach the importance of customer service first and will give technical instruction afterwards. They put new employees in the position of customers and explore their reactions, before explaining the technicalities. They recognize that inward-looking, process-orientated training can lead to deeply insensitive behaviour towards customers.

Performance appraisal and promotion criteria

Which is more important: satisfying your 'real' customers (the external people who pay, directly or indirectly, for your services), or your boss (who is also your 'customer' in the sense that he/she uses your services and typically pays for them out of a departmental budget)? The fact that this question can be asked helps to justify the claim that there are sometimes conflicting priorities. Regardless of categories printed on appraisal forms, career-minded employees will soon discover what *really* counts along the promotion ladder, and will behave accordingly. If pleasing the boss is more significant than satisfying the ultimate customer, then that is what they will do.

Appraisal and promotion systems, therefore, have to send out unambiguous signals to reinforce a customer-service ethos. So far as performance review is concerned, much depends on the design of your specific system. If it's structured around the production of agreed performance-improvement objectives (to cover the next review period), it's always possible to insist that at least two of the objectives should be centrally concerned with customer care:

(1) *Improved performance from the job-holder in dealing with his/her customers* (whether internal or external); and

(2) *Improved performance from the job-holder in promoting customer-service enhancements from his/her staff, both collectively and individually.*

Don't forget the initiatives taken by organizations like Rank Xerox to build customer-service components into their performance appraisal and managerial reward systems, and to collect evidence from staff surveys, peer-group ratings, and upward appraisal.

Work organization and 'empowerment'
In the thrill-packed days of job enrichment there were many attempts to create a more satisfying work climate through increased delegation of responsibility for work planning, execution and control. Volvo's autonomous working groups and scores of other initiatives were carefully studied and copied, usually at the instigation of personnel managers who had at last found a way of reconciling a liberal conscience with industrial best practice. Most of these experiments have been abandoned, not because they incorporated false ideas about human motivation, and not only because shifting expectations will make any solution otiose after a time. The real reason was that the experiments usually lacked any commercial impetus and were therefore vulnerable

to hard-nosed management practices, especially in the two recessions of the 1980s.

Currently, by contrast, there is a rebirth of interest because senior managers can see a sound commercial link between intrinsic motivation and the delivery of customer-service benefits. As one car manufacturer once said:

'For five years I increased car productivity by coercion, but I cannot improve quality in the same way. These people have to *want* to make good cars.'

Empowerment means that front-line customer-service staff don't have to mouth centrally dictated words and phrases parrot-fashion ('Thank you for ringing the Blah Blah Hotel; Melanie speaking: how may I help you?'), but can create their own introductory messages, subject to their consistency with the preferred corporate image. Empowerment also means that customer-service staff have discretion to settle complaints immediately, without reference to supervisors, and can also agree to give customers something a little out of the ordinary if that is what they want. Empowerment doesn't happen very often in organizations like banks, insurance companies, government departments, local authorities, British Rail, and any other bureaucratic or quasi-militaristic structures where the idea of decision-making discretion at shop-floor level is anathema.

Yet, contrary to popular belief, empowerment is actually cost-effective. Research shows that when staff deal directly with complaints, they are likely to arrive at quicker, more amicable and less costly settlements than if complaints have to be channelled through a formal complaints procedure. For example, when guests of an American hotel chain were invited to fix their own compensation as restitution for their complaints, they were usually happy to settle for complimentary drinks. When Ford's Belgian operation decided to allow its dealers to resolve complaints without a cost limit, it found that complaints dropped by 75 per cent and, in addition, settlement costs were lower.

'Hygiene' factors

If Herzberg is to be believed, performance is a combination of 'motivators' and 'hygiene' factors. The 'motivators' are centrally concerned with the job itself; they reflect the opportunities for ego–stroking, personal satisfaction and professional challenge that the work supplies. Empowerment is the translation of these 'motivators' which enable the individual to perform at his or her best. The 'hygiene' factors, on the other hand, supply the foundation or springboard from which work performance can be improved. They include financial rewards, working conditions, the quality of supervision, coaching and training, the security surrounding the job, and the status of the work both within the organization and so far as the external world is concerned.

What this means, for customer–service people, is that the 'hygiene' elements have to be in place *before* they are likely to display personal commitment to what they do. According to studies carried out by Ashridge Management College, the specific 'hygiene' factors particularly relevant to customer–service people include:

- A reasonable level of satisfaction with pay, status and working conditions
- Strong support for front–line roles from other organizational employees at all levels
- Conviction that top management puts the customer first
- A sense of team identity associated with customer service, coupled with the belief that they are members of a winning team

- Confidence based on adequate and comprehensive training.

The Ashridge research also points to a couple of specific 'motivators':

- Regular, frequent *feedback from the customer* about the perceived quality of service they receive
- Adequate *recognition (financial and non-financial)* from management.

Enhancing the status of front-line customer-contact staff

Typically, people reflect the respect they themselves receive from others. If we get respect from the people we live with, the people we work with, and the people we work for – then we respect ourselves. This is our old friend the ego at work again.

If we respect ourselves, then in turn we're more likely to respect those we meet and deal with. Some of those people will be our customers: we might treat them better, and get better treatment from them, if we have some self-respect.

By contrast, if we are denied respect as individuals then we will generate negative and defensive attitudes – and it's difficult not to communicate these negative attitudes to others. The position is made worse if we already had negative attitudes about ourselves, and low self-esteem, before moving into a front-line customer-service scenario. Maybe we acquired these negative attitudes as a result of parental indifference, lack of achievement, and educational starvation. Whatever the causes, such people can give a hard time to organizations when put in customer-service roles.

An organization that regards its front-line staff as the bottom of the heap cannot grumble if they serve its customers badly. Yet this is precisely the situation in many companies:

- Customer-contact people are on the lowest rung of the hierarchical ladder
- They have few qualifications and limited promotion prospects
- They have generally joined the organization for reasons unconnected with commitment to the organization's goals.

'Being nice to the public' may be a feature of their subordinate position, but they may feel the need *not* to be nice, in order to assert their independence as individuals. After all, servility is a bigger threat to people who feel they are seen as servants, than to people who clearly are not.

Of course, the behaviour of front-line customer-service staff may not go so far as to be openly hostile, since this could excite retaliation and, eventually, retribution; but they can be 'nice' in such a way as to make it clear that beneath the polite veneer they are seething with apathy. Hotel receptionists who parrot the words 'Thank you for ringing the Blah Blah Hotel; Melanie speaking; how may I help you?' in a patently insincere sing-song are precisely a case in point.

So: if you want your front-line staff to serve customers well, they must *know* that they and their work are respected and appreciated. This goes further than the occasional pat on the head, which is patronizing. There must be genuine consultation and involvement on decisions that affect them, and all the signals they receive from the organization must be in the same direction. Most people are bright enough to perceive the hypocrisy when on the one hand they're told how vital they are to the success of the company, yet on the other hand are given dowdy, ill-fitting uniforms to wear.

Creating reward systems that work
First, let's outline the general principles, then put some flesh on them with specific cases, ideas and examples.

- ## What to reward?

  The key point is that you have to reward behaviour and actions that you want to be repeated (and maybe even intensified). So the reward must be linked directly and closely with the behaviour/actions/results that you want to see happen again, so that the recipient sees the connection. Further, if the reward process is made conspicuous then others can see the connection as well.

- ## Reward results more than effort

  Remember that customer service is ultimately about increasing profit, which is the only result that matters in the long run. So customer-service actions that generate results (like complimentary letters from happy customers, additional purchases, top-of-league positions in competitive tables, or bottom-line benefits) should take precedence over cases where individuals have tried hard but not delivered the goods, so to speak.

There are some exceptions to this principle. With reward systems for sales representatives, a situation can arise where the same person wins more or less everything. This can be depressing for others whose performance has improved significantly but who cannot attain the achievement levels of the permanent victor; some will not even make the effort to reach the goal of, say, a free weekend in Paris; and the top-performer may effortlessly walk away with the incentives every time. Repetitive scenarios of this kind are a turn-off for a lot of people whose performance you would like to improve: sometimes it's preferable to devise rewards based on, say, percentage improvements rather than absolute figures. Individuals and groups starting from a low base then have a chance to achieve recognition for their *efforts*, although it could be argued that a 30 per cent enhancement is, in itself, a very creditable *result*.

So it's clear that being dogmatic about results rather than effort could get us into trouble when the goal is improved customer service and customer delight. What we must avoid at all costs, is a pattern where the same people win recognition all the time.

- *Reward efforts and achievements that directly support specific customer-service goals*

This will keep the organization's eye on the ball. If you've clearly outlined a vision incorporating positive performance standards, then movement towards these standards has to be a central issue for the reward and recognition process. Rewarding other things could deflect attention away from the central, overriding purposes of the exercise.

- *Reward critical performance rather than routine tasks*

If your organization is ever to achieve the competitive edge, it will only do so by becoming special (to its customers) and by generating customer delight; the routine will generate customer satisfaction, which is good but not good enough. Critical performance means exceptional service of some kind, where an employee has driven 100 miles out of his way, and in his own time, to deliver a vital spare to your industrial customer. As an organization, you may have difficulty in learning about these cases, because often the people who behave in this fashion are the last to publicize their contribution. It takes a powerful communication system, involving first-line managers, to ensure that service triumphs can become known, acknowledged, recognized and celebrated.

Critical performance also means the production of great ideas and, better still, their effective implementation. Critical performance can mean positive treatment of customer complaints, significant breakthroughs in interdepartmental co-operation generating teamwork noticeable to the customer, and little extras which make all the difference in promoting customer goodwill. Anything out of the ordinary that benefits customers, in fact: make sure you have procedures for discovering about such incidents as soon as they've occurred. It makes sense to have a secondary reward system for first-line managers who can legitimately claim some of the credit for the superlative performance of their people, because that will help to bring the news to you (on the grounds that first-line managers will see something in it for them if they broadcast the successes of their own staff; far too often managers will actively suppress stories of achievement if they fear that their more talented and innovative people are likely to be taken away from them).

Another technique for encouraging upward feedback about customer-service triumphs is to condition managers to ask each of their subordinates for 'one-victory-a-week' anecdotes: you don't have to make it too institutionalized, but simply have a campaign every so often.

● *Reward performance that sets a good example for others*
For this to happen, of course, the reward has to be made in public, or has to be publicized, and the reason why it sets a good example has to be spelt out in capital letters. In this way you not only reinforce the behaviour in the person who is the direct recipient of the reward, but you also generate a spin-off impact for others.

● *When to reward?*
If the reward is to have the desired effect (encouraging the action that inspired it to be repeated), then it must be administered as soon after the original behaviour as possible: preferably the same day and certainly the same week. So rapid feedback procedures are essential, together with a climate in which individuals, first-line

managers and management generally are conscious of
the vital need to celebrate success, and are therefore prepared to give priority to the celebration process.

The timing of the reward can also be linked to opportunities for improving employee performance on a
wider basis, for reinforcing customer-service commitments to the outside world, and for upholding
organizational standards. If these objectives are to be
achieved, the reward has to be presented with some
ceremony (in a few instances, the ceremony *is* the reward), and organizing a ceremony takes time. Not that
much time: taking the team to the pub at Friday lunch-
time can be arranged in less than 24 hours. It's the
national award presentations that take a couple of days
longer to get off the ground.

● *Reward in public rather than in private*
According to David Freemantle (*Incredible Customer
Service – The final test;* Maidenhead: McGraw-Hill,
1993), 'A cheque for £100 sent impersonally through
the post is far less effective as a reward than £100 spent
on a celebration at which an intrinsically worthless
piece of paper (a certificate) is handed out in style.' Dispensing rewards in public, too, helps accomplish your
purpose of reinforcing positive customer-service behaviour not only for the person who earned the reward
in the first place, but also for others who could earn
similar benefits for themselves.

Of course, the exhortation about rewarding people in
public should not be taken to mean that private, one-to-
one recognition and appreciation are a waste of time.
Surely the ideal is a combination of personal thanks and
public endorsement: use one style without the other and
you're not maximizing the opportunities. Even if the
time-scale and the situation don't easily permit you to
reward in public, then the next best thing is to make

sure that your 'public' knows that someone has been re-warded. This can be done by sending round notices telling everyone what's happened, who did well, and how they were rewarded; you can benefit from such notices yourself if copies go to the senior management with your name (as the reward donor) on them, as well as the name(s) of the recipient(s). Other approaches, on a more localized basis, include designing the reward itself so that its presence announces the fact that somebody's achievement has been recognized. Cakes, bottles of wine, meals out for two at a local restaurant, are all appropriate possibilities.

- *Start by rewarding frequently*

If people haven't been rewarded before then they'll take time to get used to it. In British organizations the virtual absence of any reward and recognition system is not un-common, though there may be plenty of opportunities for punishment to signal errors of omission or commis-sion. If you announce in advance that you intend to re-ward meritorious performance in the field of customer service, there will be those who don't believe you; some will be cynical; some will put you to the test (you shouldn't mind this: what it will mean is that such people will deliberately put themselves out for a customer, then sit back to see whether they receive any-thing; so customer service has been improved already!). You'll have to work hard to overcome scepticism, apathy or hostility, and you certainly can't expect the idea of rewards for enhancing customer service to be universally welcomed.

Frequently rewarding, therefore, will help to deal with objections and overcome inertia. It will help the customer-service culture to become embedded in your organization. It will reinforce key behaviours, and demonstrate your focus on the front-line staff rather than on those who (however valuable) are more remote from the customer interface.

● *Gradually require better performance before rewarding*
As standards improve, you won't need to reward the
things that you rewarded last year, because they will
now be taken for granted. Don't forget that what
you're rewarding is *critical performance*, not routine
tasks, yet today's routine task was once yesterday's
critical innovation.

● *Be specific and sincere about what is being rewarded*
We recommend the use of this simple four-step process
for improving employee self-esteem and performance
(taken from Roger Tunks: *Fast Track to Quality*; New
York: McGraw-Hill, 1992), especially in any face-to-
face scenario.

(1) **Thanks:** Say 'Thank you' in some form or other
for the employee's contribution;
(2) **Specific:** Describe the specific behaviour that
earned recognition for the individual;
(3) **Benefit:** State how it benefits you, your department, or the organization;
(4) **Thanks:** Give an overall statement, once again, of
appreciation (much as you might when writing a
letter that begins with gratitude and closes with a
further statement along the same lines).

Tunks claims that his Fast-Track TSBT Formula for
employee recognition is a very powerful tool for building self-esteem and improvement, subject to the following rules:

(1) *Be sincere:* never offer a TSBT in a flippant, casual
way as if you're going through the motions;
(2) *Offer it soon:* TSBT should be offered as soon as
possible after the event occurs. The longer the
delay, the more diminished the impact and sincerity;
(3) *Focus on behaviour:* correct behaviour leads to correct results. If you reinforce specific behaviours,

employees will repeat these behaviours and their results will improve;

(4) *Recognize effort:* If you wait for final, bottom-line results to appear before offering TSBT to anyone, you (and they) may have to wait, a long, long time. On the contrary, TSBT reinforcements will help to grow results by giving direction to customer-service change.

● *Don't let reward systems become a boring routine*

As soon as the reward system becomes a routine, the process becomes devalued: it's viewed as a chore, the donors don't have their hearts in it any more, and the recipients wonder what they've done to deserve being chosen as 'Employee of the Month'. Spontaneous expressions of such success are far better than mechanistic rituals run by the personnel function. 'To reward successful employees and teams,' says Freemantle, 'there must be an element of surprise, of excitement, of elation.'

So managers must use their imagination to devise rewards that are effective in achieving what they set out to do. That often means, in itself, that any given reward must be different from what has gone before. With rewards, boredom sets in rapidly: if you give someone a reward identical to that dispensed elsewhere a little while before, there is a sense of let-down, even if the reward is something quite desirable. However, the variations don't have to be that significant: a meal for two at an upmarket Chinese restaurant can be offered again as a meal for two at a French restaurant, and so forth.

It's quite helpful to generate some ideas (through brainstorming) for non-pecuniary ways of recognizing above-average achievement in the field of customer service. In a recent exercise, this author, working with a group of executives from the financial services sector, generated over 50 useable ideas involving no cost at all or very limited expenditure. If people in the insurance business can think this creatively, then anyone can. What's worth remembering, too, is that with a limited budget it's preferable to keep the value of each reward low, but to broaden the net to include as many real achievers as possible. In this way (nearly) everyone can be a winner, and the psychological benefits are spread widely.

- *You don't have to wait for the organization to tell you what to do*

If you're a manager interested in improving customer service in the field – whether internal or external – for which you're responsible, you don't have to wait for your organization formally to adopt a 'policy' on the subject. The best managers simply get off their backsides and start doing it. Often the argument that 'we're awaiting policy guidance' is nothing more than a feeble excuse for continued inertia and complacency.

- *Rewards have to be geared to the requirements of the recipient, not the donor*

If you offer somebody something they don't want (a Chinese meal for a couple who don't like eating out), then, not surprisingly, you won't get anything much in the way of future performance improvement. So rewards have to be structured sensitively, perhaps with 'cafeteria' options so that recipients can select something genuinely meeting their preferences. This applies with equal force to organizations, where tailored approaches are typically more successful. Different strategies are needed, depending on the type of activity, whether its customers are internal or external, whether there are large numbers of customers or a few, the characteristics of the people in the organization, the amount of money, time and other resources available, and so on. For some organizations, dispensing 'gold stars' will be highly effective; for others it would cause hilarity, cynicism and embarrassment.

- *Use the full spectrum of reward categories: recognition, symbols and tangible benefits*

There's no obvious advantage to you in depriving yourself of opportunities for rewarding across all three groups. At the same time, if the potential recipients are likely to respond best to, say, recognition ('Well done' and 'Thank you'), then it may be unnecessary to gild the lily with additional 'benefits' that produce few returns. What this suggests is that, before beginning a reward scheme, it's useful to ask customer-service staff what types of reward will motivate them most.

Recent surveys suggest that *recognition* for a job well done is often sufficient motivation, provided it's done in accordance with the Fast-Track TSBT Formula discussed above. 'Thank you' and 'Well done' are quite enough for some people, especially if nobody has shown them any appreciation before. Others may respond positively to seeing their names in print, receiving a personal visit from a genuinely senior manager (better yet, the chairman or CEO), a hand-written note, an extra half-day off, some company products, and so forth. It's important to keep people interested by constant variation of the recognition media offered: too much of anything and it becomes devalued or routine.

The use of *symbols* is closely linked to the act of recognition. Symbols of achievement may be very small – a bunch of flowers, a special parking place, some above-average items of desk furniture – but must be visible to others as well as to the direct recipient. Displayed symbols of attainment will also incorporate certificates, plaques and diplomas acquired as a result of (successful) completion of training programmes. These can be equally helpful in impressing external customers in reception or waiting areas.

Because it's unlikely that recognition rewards and symbolic benefits will be adequate by themselves (indeed, some more cynical employees will think that you have deliberately confined your incentive system to non-pecuniary items because you're too mean to offer anything more substantial), then *tangible rewards* should enter the frame.

The danger of relying too much on money is that it takes progressively larger sums to influence behaviour. Moreover, monetary rewards are visible only to the recipient, unless he or she boasts about them, so the spin-off impact is non-existent. It's far more desirable to spend money on options that (a) keep the momentum going, (b) have a conspicuous component so that others can see what is happening, and (c) generate some excitement because of their originality. Individual prizes might include mystery weekends, use of a chauffeur-driven Rolls-Royce for a day, free tickets to a desired event – the list can be endless (and creating the list supplies a suitable opportunity for brainstorming).

- *Keep the balance between individual rewards and team/ group rewards*

If you reward only individual performance, you encourage people to compete against each other. This is fine, you may think; that's exactly what we want them to do, because out of competition springs superior performance. Well, yes, up to a point, but there are potential downsides to competition which you don't hear so much about in the literature, and which don't get articulated even when managers are speaking their minds.

First, there are two ways of winning a battle. One way is to do better than your opponents. *The other way is to make sure your opponents do less well than you do.* Thus a concentrated focus on unreconstructed individualism can set employees against each other to the point where

winning the competitive battle becomes more important than meeting the customer's needs. Individuals start
playing political games, even sabotage, all counter-
productive so far as the organization's key purposes are
concerned.

Second, competition can generate some peculiar processes in which people take advantage of the rules in
order to fudge the numbers. In a sales incentive scheme,
products may be promoted ruthlessly in the run-up to
the scheme's deadline date, regardless of the rejected de-
liveries or returned goods occurring in the next month.
Sales representatives will study the fine print in order to
ensure that they maximize their rewards through minimal effort. A great deal of (ultimately unproductive)
effort is expended on activities that distort the corporate
results but which, from a self-interested view-point,
achieve competitive advantage only for individuals.

If you reward groups, then much the same consider-
ations apply. Previously co-operative relationships can
be damaged beyond repair. Shift teams, forced into
competition with each other, may deliberately make
things awkward for their successors or, more subtly,
will collaborate among themselves to thwart management's purposes.

Creating a teamwork culture is fine where organizations operate through branch offices or retail shops:
each unit can become a team, co-operating wholeheart-
edly to make the operation successful both internally
and so far as customers are concerned. Teamwork has
more obvious snags when it means, in large organizations, that (say) the sales department or the finance
people operate as teams. If a collection of people is to
become more than a number of separate individuals, so
that it is welded into a team in the genuine sense of the

word, then one of the factors promoting cohesiveness within the group will be the members' consciousness of superiority to the world outside. It is also well known that group cohesion is much stronger when groups and teams see themselves as the beleaguered victims of an obsessive enemy. So it wouldn't be unusual if the (strongly cohesive) sales department came to think of the finance function as one of its enemies, followed closely by the marketers. This is not a recipe for effective customer service.

There is no panacea for resolving these dilemmas. Most organizations use a judicious combination of individual and group recognition schemes, but with the emphasis tailor-made to the needs, structure and culture of the company. Inter-branch and inter-store competitions can work well, especially if combined with efforts to single out high-performing individuals (who may not necessarily come from the winning branches or stores). What has to be remembered, however, is that external customers are seldom interested in whether they're shopping at this year's winning branch unit. What concerns them is whether they're receiving competent attention and service, and they couldn't care less whether they're getting it from a top-performing shop or the one at the bottom of the heap.

It's noticeable, in fact, that organizations advertise only the achievements of their winning units. You may see a framed plaque on the wall of your building society branch claiming that they are 'Southern Region Branch of the Year', but you'll never see plaques to tell you that 'Our position is 98th out of 100 branches'. Perhaps that would be too much of a hostage to fortune, though if the plaque went on to say something like 'We aim to significantly improve our position next year, and that's why our customer service is so much better' then we would sit up and be impressed.

6

ACHIEVING SUSTAINABLE COMPETITIVE ADVANTAGE THROUGH CUSTOMER SERVICE

The Holy Grail is the acquisition of a competitive advantage which

- supplies some perceived benefits to the external customer; and
- can be sustained over time.

Anyone can produce a competitive advantage, but it will be short-lived if your competitors can match it or even better it. Reduce your prices (as supermarkets will sometimes do) and others will do the same. Nobody is better off, apart from the consumer, and possibly the supermarket chain that can persuade customers (whether it's true or not) that their price reductions are deeper and more wide-ranging than anybody else's.

Without a competitive advantage of some sort, there is no reason for you still to be in business. The conscious search for a competitive advantage will involve investment of managerial time and money. There is a risk that the search will be fruitless, the effort unrewarding, the outcomes unsatisfactory. The risks of such failure can be reduced by avoiding the search for a competitive advantage. However, without a competitive advantage there are no risks at all, because failure is guaranteed.

Competitive advantage relies upon differentiation. Low price is one form of differentiation, but it is often unsustainable except for one or two market-dominant organizations able to reap full benefit from economies of scale. Further, low price is often equated with low margins: the ability to charge higher prices is linked to higher profitability (as Sainsburys and subsequently Tesco have found by repositioning themselves in the marketplace). Organizations relying on low prices for their competitive advantage are vulnerable to existing or new-entry competitors which may not have scale economies but may achieve other cost breakthroughs by using, for example, their own distribution systems (created for other purposes) or point-of-sale outlets, and by technological progress.

Most damning of all for those organizations differentiating themselves through low prices is the fact that customers will often equate low prices with low quality, whether or not there is any justification for this supposed relationship. For some commodities in particular, the equation 'low price = low quality' is not so apparent, but even supermarket petrol has been vilified because it does not contain the detergents used by the major oil companies.

Differentiation is dangerous, then, if it depends exclusively on price. So, leaving price on one side, we could define differentiation as *the provision of something unique that is valuable to the customer (other than price)*. The benefits of differentiation, especially if it can be sustained, are:

- It allows the organization to command a premium price (and therefore to secure higher margins)
- The organization can sell more of its products or services at a given price
- The organization will enjoy greater customer loyalty during cyclical or seasonal downturns
- If the organization moves from a monopoly position to a competitive environment (like corporate-service functions submitting themselves to competitive tendering, or newly privatized public-sector departments), then previously tied customers

may willingly continue to buy whatever the organization supplies.

The one caveat to the above list of advantages is that differentiation leads to superior performance only if the price premium achieved exceeds any added costs of being unique. So, if customer service is the source of differentiation, it produces no tangible gain if the extra business achieved is swallowed up by customer-service training, reward systems, incentive programmes, and other costs. This helps to remind us of one of the recurrent themes in this book, namely, that the name of the game with customer service is enhanced profit (or increased survival chances in the case of non-competitive organizations). Customer service is a means to an end, not an end to itself.

Organizations of whatever type (whether private sector, public sector, or third sector) can differentiate themselves in a variety of ways. Note that for any of these differentiating factors to be worthwhile they must (a) be perceived by the customer, and (b) be perceived as beneficial.

- Product/service features (seen as 'benefits') by customers and/or users
- Product/service performance
- Methods of delivery
- Delivery times and frequency
- Intensity and methods of product/service promotion (e.g., use of direct mail, advertising, mail order, market research)
- Quality of sales force and methods of selling (e.g., home-service visits versus reliance on brokers in the financial services sector)
- After-sales service
- The skills and experience of the staff employed in providing the product/services offered by the organization

- The technology employed in the product/service provision process
- Procedures governing the actions of the staff (e.g., the nature and number of sales calls, frequency of inspection, the nature and frequency of feedback sought from customers)
- Speed and nature of order processing
- Mechanisms for processing and responding to complaints.

Some of these will be more significant for some businesses than for others. All of them offer scope for establishing a unique advantage for those organizations prepared to concentrate their efforts on creating it.

In reality, it is not organizations that create competitive advantage: it is *people*. All the evidence suggests that pursuing any form of competitive advantage requires a *product champion* if it is to succeed. Customer service is no different; there has to be a customer-service champion, and that person has to be the CEO or his/her equivalent in other types of structure. The head of the personnel/human resources function doesn't have enough clout; and if customer service is spear-headed by anyone in charge of marketing, sales or production, then it will be viewed as concerned solely with marketing, sales or production. Further, the heads of functions contributing from less dominant positions will be jealous of whoever is in charge of the customer-service effort. The result is lip-service commitment, reluctance to attend meetings (coupled with the eagerness to send substitutes), and the use of bureaucratic working parties as a delaying device.

Even with the CEO in charge, there is no guarantee that customer service will 'work'. Functional heads may continue to pursue their own concerns, devoting just sufficient effort to avoid charges of backsliding; and middle managers across the board may well feel threatened by talk of empowerment if it means that their status is undermined.

So the CEO has to lead by example. How can this high-sounding talk be translated into everyday action? Here are some ideas:

(1) *Role-modelling:* If Disneyland's CEO picks up litter, then so can you. If the CEO fulfils a promise to reply to all correspondence within 24 hours, then so can you. It is disastrous to the CEO's credibility if he preaches one gospel but publicly displays adherence to another.

(2) *Face-to-face communication:* The customer-service CEO devotes a lot of time to making himself personally visible to the troops (just as Montgomery did during the Second World War), by speaking at seminars and conferences, by contributing to customer-service training, and by MBWA (Managing By Wandering Around).

(3) *Company newsletters, posters and manuals:* The CEO must repeat the message constantly wherever and whenever opportunities present themselves. The more noises about customer service are made, the more likely it is that they will come to be understood and acted upon. A single advertising and PR campaign isn't enough, especially if new concepts are being sold.

(4) *Positive reinforcement:* If the CEO says he believes in customer service, then he must set customer-service standards for himself, consciously pursue feedback from customers himself, and reward those who excel in customer service.

(5) *Recruitment policies:* The CEO should persuade his personnel people to recruit only those who fit the desired culture or who are capable of adapting to it.

(6) *Promotion policies:* Key positions must be occupied

by individuals who embody the desired customer-service attitudes and behaviour. If the word spreads that non-adherence to customer-service values will inhibit careers and may even lead to people being ousted from the organization altogether, then so much the better. One or two conspicuous departures will normally be sufficient before people start to think that this time the CEO really means it.

(7) *Training:* The CEO is in a powerful position to demand that all training in the organization has a customer-service orientation. Induction training in particular is critical, with more attention to ways of meeting the expectations of customers than to compliance with the rulebook.

(8) *Equality of treatment:* Technically speaking, all organizations are supposed to be equal opportunity employers. The reality is that many are not, thereby depriving themselves of worthwhile talent on a massive scale. Discrimination also sends negative messages to customers, particularly if they include significant numbers of females. The CEO must actively intervene to undermine ignorance and prejudice (for example, against the employment of women as sales representatives in the financial services sector).

(9) *Showmanship and symbolism:* The CEO has to use modern communications technology to generate and lead roadshows, conventions and other events aimed at reinforcing the culture.

By the way, the appointment of a 'customer service director' or someone with an equally impressive title won't work either. Many years ago, Burns and Stalker showed that if an organization has a 'problem', it will not be resolved by grafting someone on to the existing structure. The individual becomes more preoccupied with ensuring his own survival, preferably by creating a department from what was originally a one-person role. The last thing he wants to do is to solve the 'problem' because in doing so he will solve himself out of a job. Fortunately, customer service is not the kind if 'problem' for which there is a single once-and-for-all cure, so perhaps a customer service director can seem to be successful simply by implementing one panacea after another. More crucial is the point that a customer service director will seldom have sufficient power and authority to make significant things happen. The CEO may give some support at the outset, especially as it will be he who authorized the appointment of the customer services director in the first place. But eventually the CEO's mind will turn to other things, it will become more difficult for the customer services director to see him, and everyone will wonder why nothing changes.

WHAT GOES WRONG?

Many organizational changes work for the first five minutes. The CEO is excited; the management team takes up the cudgels; managers further down the line may be caught up in the heat of the moment; very junior people may well see the change (whatever it is) as a long-sought opportunity to escape from the routines of a centralized and stultifying control system. The language used for managing the change can be powerful rhetoric; generous resources are made available for transmitting the message to all parts of the organization; charismatic gurus are engaged in order to motivate the masses. It doesn't matter whether the change is a customer-service programme, or a new appraisal system, or a reshuffling of responsibilities, the sequence is much the same: trumpets are blown (sometimes literally), everyone is swamped with propaganda, enthusiasm is captured, then disappointment and disillusion take over, apathy and cynicism reign once more. Now it will be even more difficult for the *next* change campaign to take off.

So does it have to be like this? The answer, of course, is an emphatic NO. It's particularly ironic, too, that the reasons for failure are so well known, yet they continue to be repeated time and time again.

1. Customer service fails to be integrated into the organizational culture

It's often the case that the management style is so deeply ingrained that a new customer-service philosophy cannot hope to succeed. The only way to break this paradigm is to replace some key senior people (who are usually 'senior' not only in the hierarchy but also in the sense that they are the older, more 'experienced' members of the organization). The newcomers will be more uninhibited, less respectful about established ways of doing things, and have a greater investment in introducing change.

Here are some common factors often found in organizations with a poor record for customer service (some readers may care to reflect on the relevance of these factors in their own organization and in organizations – airlines, hotels, railways – to which they relate as customers).

- *Complacency and arrogance:* deep scepticism about the value of studying the competition, the need for an explicit corporate strategy, and the benefits of training (especially management training)
- *Conservatism:* lack of receptiveness to new ideas, resistance to change, and hostility to new technology
- *Production orientation:* strong suspicions about the value of marketing
- *Functionalism:* adherence to functional and departmental boundaries, with a consequential focus on empire-building and inter-functional rivalries
- *Status and seniority:* high ranking organizational employees are held in awe; distracting issues like

company cars and executive dining rooms are
thought to be extremely important

- *A secretive, closed attitude to information*: many documents and internal communications are classified as
'confidential'

- *Tolerance of inadequate achievements:* excuses for poor
customer-service performance are supplied, and are
acceptable. In particular, it is rare to take decisive
action to deal with very senior management who
have ceased to perform adequately or who have developed behaviour problems such as alcoholism

- *Scepticism about people:* organizational effectiveness
is not thought to be anything to do with the motivation of staff, their commitment, their involvement
in decision-making and the leadership shown by
management

- *Rules and procedures treated as ends in themselves:* strict
adherence to job description boundaries and a 'not
invented here' attitude to questions of individual responsibility for performance

- *Masculine culture:* lip service paid to equality of
opportunity for women, and very few in key
management jobs

- *Insularity:* a tendency to treat the organization as if it
exists for the benefit of its members, linked with
hostility towards customers, who are often quite
literally seen as the enemy; ignorance of and little
curiosity about broad trends in the business environment.

2. Lack of support from senior management in terms of on-going commitment

After the initial flurry of activity, senior managers
become distracted by other (short-term) business problems. This is particularly widespread where such 'problems' include the pressure to meet bottom-line targets
(customer-service changes, by contrast, seldom generate visible outputs in the immediate aftermath of their

implementation). If senior managers change their tone, it is little wonder that middle managers do the same.

3. Staff are cynical

This isn't surprising: some of them have seen it all before. Others haven't, but think they have: they take their cue from more battle-weary peers. Sometimes the staff are cynical because it is clear that management doesn't believe what it's saying either: they are mouthing the right words, but their sincerity is, at best, muted.

As we've already argued elsewhere, the attitude of staff to a proposed change is to ask themselves 'What's in it for us?' If they come to the view that the effort of moving with the change (in other words, consciously improving their customer-service behaviour)will not be recognized, then they will behave like the rational creatures they are – by continuing to act in the way to which they've grown accustomed. This isn't cynicism at all, in fact: it's what any sensible person should do if they subscribe (however unknowingly) to Darwin's survival-of-the-fittest theory. However, it *looks* like cynicism to people (senior managers) who are driven by self-interested goals of their own.

Cynicism can be undermined if an appropriate combination of reward systems is introduced, thereby changing the calculations involved in 'What's in it for us?' Cynicism has also to be addressed through consistent leadership and role-modelling, plus careful methods for promoting genuine 'ownership' (not just a sense of ownership) among staff.

4. The customer-service philosophy does not produce quick results

Of course, improving customer service seldom does yield an immediate return, so 'quick-win' expectations are mistaken. This does not stop people from having them, however, or from reacting badly when the expectations are not fulfilled.

It's certainly important to give wide publicity for all victories, to demonstrate that progress is being made. The momentum can be sustained only if the publicity is continuous and the rewards permanently promoted.

5. Training in customer service is seen as a one-off exercise.

It may be that the organization takes customer service to its bosom, spends large sums on company-wide indoctrination and then assumes the issue is resolved. Nothing could be further from the truth.

Moreover, training in customer service has limited pay-off if the training messages are confined to pious generalities and unarguable platitudes. What people at the sharp end, involved in countless 'moments of truth' with external customers, want to know is precisely how they are now expected to act. What must they say and do differently? How much power does this 'empowerment' notion actually convey?

6. The customer-service initiative is all about training and nothing else

Customer service will not improve if the initiative is seen to be inspired by some adventurous training department. The problem here, even if the training has the ear of the CEO, is that there are usually other more powerful groups in the organization that may not want to buy into customer service. People will 'volunteer' for the training programmes (if the CEO tells them to), but any subsequent attempts to change things will not be reinforced by managers who have a greater investment in the status quo. Indeed, it is noticeable in situations like this that the delegates for customer-service training are invariably junior personnel, while their managers keep away, not wishing to be tainted by these new-fangled concepts and gimmicks.

7. Attention is concentrated on external customers but internal relationships remain just as bad as they were before.

'Them and us' barriers can effectively scupper any faint hope that overall customer service could be enhanced. If the customer service 'chain' is ignored, if people are more concerned with job preservation and adherence to procedures than in meeting the expectations of the clients who ultimately pay, then external customers are unlikely to benefit at all.

8. Absence of performance improvement feedback

There's plenty of research to support the belief that if people don't get feedback about how well they're doing, their performance suffers through increasing anxiety and uncertainty. That is certainly true of customer service. If the employees get no information about progress, then they will think there hasn't been any, and they will become demoralized. If achievements and customer-service 'victories' aren't acknowledged, celebrated and rewarded, then people (not unnaturally) will wonder why they should continue to make the effort.

9. Quality improvement teams are bogged down in detail

If improving customer services includes the creation of one-off project groups to tackle specific issues, or functional teams set up on a permanent basis, these activities have to be led by individuals who have a strong single-minded focus on results. All too often, groups spend most of their time:

(a) Demanding more detailed information on current performance standards;

(b) Critically analysing such information after it's been gathered;

(c) Concentrating on minor details;

(d) Blaming everyone else in the organization for not doing their jobs properly; and

(e) Arguing that their own performance cannot improve until they receive more resources (higher pay, more space, better equipment, extra people).

Where such behaviour patterns occur, then of course customer service will not improve – indeed, standards may even fall because so many front-line people are away at quality-improvement meetings.

10. Absence of sustained pressure from on high

We've already stressed this point. British management is notorious for its dilettantism, its amateurishness, its search for the quick (and preferably inexpensive) fix, its eagerness for panaceas, its enthusiasm for discarding new techniques when they don't product instant improvements. The position is dramatically summarised by the opening of *You Won't Do It*, a report produced by the National Quality Campaign's Pacific Basin Study Mission in 1987:

'We asked him why Japanese companies had thrown open their factories, talked frankly to us about their techniques, shown us the secrets of their success. "Because," he said, "it would take ten years to get where we are now and by that time we shall be even further ahead. And besides," he smiled, "we know you won't do it!"'

HOW CAN WE GET IT RIGHT?

Don't forget that in this chapter we're talking about the ways of generating a sustainable competitive advantage from customer service. Many of the points that follow may seem obvious, even self-evident, but if they are then it's curious that so few of them are taken seriously.

1. Continuous improvement through bringing the customer into the organization

Continuous improvement itself isn't enough because it can mean nothing more than getting better at what we do now. Concentrating on doing more of what we do now – working harder rather than working smarter – is pointless if what we do now is not what today's and tomorrow's customers want from us. Bringing the customer into the equation can transform the continuous improvement process by making it both relevant and meaningful.

Working with customer feedback means finding out what products or services our customers need, and ways in which our products and services can be extended to new groups of customers. Edward Heath neatly summed up what customer-orientation really means, quoting Deng-Xiaoping's remark:

'The Americans and the Europeans come to us offering splendid goods and inquiring how much we want to buy . . . the Japanese approach is to ask us what we want, how much we can afford to pay and then produce the goods.'

This helps us to clarify two aspects of quality that are immediately significant for customer service. First, in our society we are apt to think that a Rolls is quality whereas a Mini is not. No so: a small car with the design and reliability that people will buy and recommend is a quality car. Secondly, quality is not found in a fixed set of features for a product or service, but rather in a relationship with customers where their needs are established, and then re-established over and over again.

2. Continuous creativity in moving ahead of customer needs and expectations

Nishikawa (*Journal of Long Range Planning*, Vol 22, No 4, 1989) points out that 'the most important factor in understanding consumers' attitudes and in building marketing strategy is not logical analysis, but creative action.' Responding to customers' needs is acting too late for successful marketing: in order to forecast the future, organizations require creativity rather than responsiveness, challenge rather than passivity. Market research (for new products and services) is highly suspect because of certain features of customer psychology:

(a) *Indifference:* customers often provide negative responses to (ideas for) new products/services simply because they are indifferent to something they have not thought about or tried before;

(b) *Absence of responsibility:* people will say more or less anything when responding to market research surveys, often out of a desire to please the researcher. As Nishikawa says, *customers are most sincere when spending rather than talking*;

(c) *Conservative attitudes:* most customers choose conventional and familiar goods/services; only about three to five per cent of all customers are innovative people;

(d) *Vanity:* customers will put on a good appearance, for example, by not admitting that cheapness was the major reason for a purchase decision;

(e) *Insufficient information:* researchers (and organizations) often approach customers with information and ideas seen from the seller's rather than the customer's point of view.

3. Promising something definite and then supplying it

Far too many organizations won't commit themselves to anything ('we can't promise') or commit themselves to something and then fail to deliver. You could achieve an enviable competitive advantage simply by developing a reputation for sticking to your promises and for entering into commitments that maximize the benefits for your customers (or, if you're in the repair and maintenance business, minimize their inconvenience). Organizations can get business by promising service; they retain business by keeping their promises.

4. Putting resources into telephone manners
The importance of positive telephone treatment is neatly recognized in *How to Turn Customer Service into Customer Sales* by Bernard Katz (Aldershot: Gower Publishing, 1987). Katz tape-recorded telephone enquiries to ten organizations: British Airways, British Rail, Alpine Double Glazing, Crittall Windows, Thermobreak, Bristol Street Motors, Oxford Motors, Kwik-Fit Euro, an electricity board, and the Anglian Water Board. The taped calls are played to delegates attending customer-service programmes, but beforehand everyone is asked to rate, on a scale of 0–10, their expectations of the level of service that will be provided. Having listened to the calls, participants are asked to rate the same organization again: what responses do they now expect, in the light of what they have just heard?

Every time the exercise is used, the level of expectation for organizations upgraded by the group rises by an average of 1 point.

Downgraded organizations drop by an average of 3 points.

We believe this exercise to reflect, in microcosm, all customer expectations of the service they will receive – yet it stems from a single, sometimes brief and sometimes apparently insignificant transaction.

Doing it right involves four general principles and ten specific techniques. The general principles first:

(1) **Good communication.** Effective communication occurs when messages sent by one party are

received by someone else without distortion. Both parties must have the same frame of reference; they must agree to use common units and scales; they should check frequently to confirm that meanings are clear and as intended; and the language used should be simple rather than complicated, with short rather than long sentences.

(2) **Speaking clearly.** Everyone without an organic or psychological impediment can speak clearly, if they want to. Here are some **Do**'s and **Don't**s.

Do:

- Hold the mouthpiece correctly
- Keep it at the right distance
- Breathe normally
- Use short sentences
- Speak slowly
- Pause occasionally.

Don't:

- Mumble
- Eat, drink or smoke while talking
- Shout
- Use jargon
- Interrupt yourself or others.

(3) **Empathy.** If you're empathetic, you are capable of seeing the situation from the other's point of view. This is quite different from being sympathetic, which means being sorry for someone without necessarily understanding what they're making such a fuss about.

I'm demonstrating *empathy* if I say 'You look as if you could do with a drink'; I'm showing *sympathy* if I offer to buy you one.

When dealing with people over the phone, empathy is the skill of understanding (and predicting) how the person being spoken to is reacting to (or is likely to react to) what is being said – and then modifying the transaction so that the reaction is more likely to be the desired one.

(4) **Courtesy.** Irrespective of the nature of the phone call, courtesy should be an integral part of the process. Lack of courtesy is often an emphatic indicator of the emotional feelings of the speaker: letting these feelings show is an exercise in self-indulgence which could easily be counter-productive.

Now the ten specific techniques:

(1) **Answer your telephone within five seconds or three rings.**
Customers will regard this delay as acceptable. When customer-service programmes are initiated, they often generate a manic rush to answer all phones more or less as soon as they ring, but this isn't necessary. Callers like to take a few seconds to compose themselves after they've dialled the number: from their viewpoint the response can be *too* efficient if you're speaking before they've even heard your phone ring.

(2) **Answer any unattended telephones within your reach.**
It's an unforgivable sin to ignore ringing phones, whether or not it's your lunch-hour. Any sensible working arrangement will include staggered break times for the middle of the day, plus automatic diversion systems for incoming enquiries.

(3) **Smile as you pick up the receiver.**

This may sound daft, but the idea is to get you into the right frame of mind so that you're more likely to be friendly and courteous. Smiling at the end of the day is harder than smiling first thing in the morning, but with practice smiling can become a worthwhile habit.

(4) **Give the incoming call your undivided attention.**

Don't try to combine answering the phone with something else, like signalling your drinks order to a beckoning colleague, or playing battleships on your PC, or doodling on your newspaper. The fact that you are distracted (and therefore not paying attention) is likely to transmit itself to callers, especially if they hear you speaking to someone else.

(5) **Begin with a word of greeting.**

All right, so saying 'hello', or 'good morning' may not be particularly businesslike, but at least such words make it sound as if you're pleased to be speaking to someone. What's equally important is that the caller may not 'hear' your opening word(s) anyway, because of line clicks or the fact that they're not in a listening mode the moment the call begins, so it's preferable that these first words are, in a sense, dispensable. For this reason it's not desirable to start by saying your name, or the name of your department or organization, because such details are more critical.

(6) **Identify (yourself and) your department or organization.**

When the call comes through a switchboard, giving the name of your department may be sufficient, and certainly the organization's or department's name should be said before your own. If you're likely to receive calls from external customers, then it's more helpful if your department has a name that makes sense to them. For an insurance company to say 'OB Accounts' when picking up the phone is particularly hopeless if you're ringing them about your standing order.

The actual name of the person answering the phone is not relevant all the time. It's not applicable, for example, when someone is asking the price of theatre seats, seeking a telephone number from directory enquiries, or needing the day's weather forecast. On the other hand, the name is important if the caller is likely to expect action to arise from the call. The name then becomes a point of contact (and, of course, a focus for complaint if the expected action does not happen).

For most purposes, a first name and a surname will be best; contrary to the expectations of most hotels, a first name on its own doesn't sound more friendly and intimate, particularly as the person thus identified is unlikely to be referring to *you* by your first name.

(7) **Establish the caller's needs.**
Find out by questioning: open questions (beginning with interrogative words) rather than closed (yes/no) questions. Sometimes the needs are readily volunteered by the caller, but not everyone is articulate, not everyone has worked out clearly in advance what it is they want, and not everyone has got through to the right person anyway. Questions should pinpoint the general area of help needed in the first instance, and then gradually focus on to the more localized and specific issues.

Key information from the caller should be written down on a pad, so that the same questions don't have to be asked twice. Many organizations have special forms, or use appropriate hardware/software incorporating VDUs or PCs. Such systems can work brilliantly if data about the caller's connection with the organization can be readily portrayed on the screen.

(8) **Provide the information or help required.**
Telling the customer what you're doing, while you're doing it, helps to reassure the customer that something is happening. It's certainly preferable to unexplained silences. If it's necessary for you to put the phone down, or leave your workstation for a moment, or put the caller on hold, then say so. If you're going to transfer someone to another number, you should say what you're doing and give a positive reason for doing it (if you don't, they will think you are simply passing the buck).

In the case of calling back, procedures must be very strict. Promises that are not kept are likely to mean lost business. It's best to present the customer with options ('Will you hold on, or shall I call you back?') and also to undertake to ring back within a designated period or at a specific time ('I'll contact you between 3.30 and 4, if that's going to be convenient for you').

(9) **Dealing with complaints and angry customers.**
There are three crucial guidelines. The first is to *listen*, the second is to *listen*, and the third is to *listen*. The caller who is not materially interrupted will eventually calm down, if only because of emotional exhaustion. They will now be in a more rational frame of mind, and appropriate action can be suggested, in accordance with normal customer response procedures.

The worst thing to do is to argue or challenge.

Coming a close second for irrelevance and foolishness is the eagerness to offer 'excuses' (the computer's down; half the staff are at lunch; we've just had a fire) which only irritate the customer even more. As we've said before, the customer is not interested in your problems.

(10) **Close the call.**

All customers should go away firmly convinced that the organization cares about their problem. Enquirers after information are thanked for their interest; callers seeking action must believe that they will obtain a response. It is especially important, for 'action' calls, to give and re-emphasize your name as the person to contact if anything furthers goes wrong.

When action has been promised, within an agreed deadline, but it seems inevitable that there will be further delays, then you should phone the caller to explain. Good customer relationships disintegrate rapidly when promised action fails to materialize. This one phone call will represent the difference between customer tolerance and customer anger – especially if the customer intends to take the day off work to wait indoors for your people to call.

5. Publicizing tight performance standards – and keeping to them

These are the kinds of performance criteria that will give your organization the competitive edge:

- All documents from customers requiring a response should be acknowledged within two days.
- If a full reply can't be given within the two-day deadline, then the acknowledgement will specify a final date for 'delivery' of the comprehensive answer.

- *The person to whom correspondence is addressed should reply – not somebody else on their behalf.* If customers are encouraged to write to the CEO, then the reply must originate with the CEO, not the quality control manager.

- By the same token, *customers should be given the name of someone who is responsible for looking after their business and who can answer queries on their behalf.* This someone will hardly ever be a manager or head of department because they are inevitably remote from individual cases. If necessary, the someone can be given a more impressive (and customer-related) job title: in a recent instance, this author was instrumental in changing a job-title from 'district office clerk' to 'customer services officer' in part of a financial services company where previously all policy-holder letters had gone out under the umbrella of the local branch manager, whether he/she had written it or not.

- *No customer should have to wait more than two minutes before getting attention.* If this seems far-fetched, think about the organizations that manage to achieve it, even during busy times, and those that don't. The differences don't depend on the availability of staff, but rather on the way people are used, how they are supervized, and whether someone takes action to open more service-delivery points when queues threaten the published performance standard.

6. Recruiting, selecting and training staff who have the right attitude, know what they are doing, and have the authority to do it.

For organizations dedicated to customer service, empowerment isn't just a word. It starts with recruitment, and even further back than that with the recruiters, some of whom wouldn't know the right mentality for effective customer service if it rose up and struck them violently. Having attracted staff who appear promising, they then have to be trained, not only in customer-care techniques but also in product/service knowledge. As David Freemantle says (*Incredible Customer Service: The Final Test*), 'Ignorance in front of customers is commonplace.' Staff don't know whether something is in stock or not, they don't know the price or how to calculate it, they don't know how it works or what it does, they don't know where to find other products than the ones for which they exercise (nominal) responsibility, and they don't know how to resolve problems.

It's not surprising that staff are so badly informed, because often they are given no incentives to acquire and retain information. They may even be told that if they are asked questions which they cannot answer, they should refer the customer to someone else with more experience or with more authority – someone, in other words, who is more than a Saturday person.

So if you want your staff to deliver effective customer care, then a number of things have to happen:

- They must be persuaded to take a 'total' view of customer service rather than one confined to a narrow perspective.
- They have to become familiar with what goes on in other parts of the organization, so that they can answer questions about the location of, say, other departments.
- They have to be allowed to make decisions (even decisions that involve money) without referring the customer to someone else.

7. Creating attention to detail through leadership by example.

Customer care, in the end, is about attention to detail. The better your customer service, the more noticeable it is when you get it wrong. Further, customers become more nit-picking every day: things they took for granted years ago (reliance on Black Forest Gâteau in the dessert menu) they now regard with contempt. If you get 99 of things right, but one thing wrong, it will be the wrong thing that your customers will remember, and all the rest will have done you no good at all.

Some managers are frightened of addressing the details of customer care because they don't want to appear petty-minded, and they don't like upsetting staff by criticizing small things whilst, apparently, ignoring everything else. They may take the view that nobody is perfect and some mistakes are to be expected from fallible human beings. This, in effect, was the line taken recently by the Scottish hospital which amputated the wrong testicle from a man whose left testicle had been diagnosed as cancerous. What's worse, it turned out that the diagnosis had been incorrect in the first place, so the result was what may be termed a double whammy for the poor patient. Still, as the hospital manager said, you've got to expect a few mistakes in a large organization.

In reality, our Scottish testicle-free friend would probably tell us that the search for perfection is not, and should not be, a futile process. Look at it this way. If any given employee is reliable 90 per cent of the time, then that person's output is 90 per cent reliable. If three people work as a team, each being 90 per cent reliable, then the team has 72.9 per cent reliability: more than a quarter of its results will include mistakes. If each of 1,000 people is only 90 per cent reliable, then the overall reliability of the organization is less than 50 per cent. What kind of a quality customer service is that?

So senior management, leading by example, must do these things:

- *Talk frequently to customers and staff*, praising customer service achievements, recognizing effort, and spreading the word about the organization's customer-care focus.
- *Better still, listen to customers and employees*, finding out what they think, what they value, how you could improve.
- *Introduce formal requirements for all managers to spend at least a third of their time with customers or with front-line customer-service people.*
- *Look for evidence of constant attention to customer-care improvements*, through brainstorming, team meetings, individual initiative.
- *Take action to correct mistakes/omissions of detail*, but without letting the perspective become exclusively focused on the things that go wrong.
- *Keep a beady eye on the competition*, and preferably be several steps ahead – if you keep on improving, they'll never catch up.

7

TRAINING FOR A CUSTOMER-SERVICE MENTALITY

Many organizations have spent many thousands of pounds on customer-care training from top management down to front-line staff. Much of this money has been wasted, sometimes for reasons that have little to do with the effectiveness of the training as such. As with all kinds of training, customer-care training is a dead loss if the relevant customer-service skills are not re-inforced afterwards – by reward and recognition systems, by leadership from above, by top managerial commitment, and by periodic booster doses.

Let's focus first of all on the specific causes for wasted money within the training itself. Here are some:

(1) *The training starts with front-line customer-service staff, rather than at the top.* The result is the absence of any supporting behaviour from the hierarchy – indeed, old priorities will soon re-assert themselves as supervisors and managers kill (through cynicism) initiatives from which they have been excluded.

(2) *The training starts and finishes with front-line customer-service staff,* as if they alone are responsible for the organization's customer-care performance. This approach is often accompanied by tight central controls, thus virtually eliminating the chance that front-line staff can use their initiative.

(3) *The trainers have no credibility.* If they're in-house people, they're likely to be line-manager rejects or inexperienced youngsters, full of theoretical concepts but empty of practical tools.

(4) *Customer-service training is seen as a one-off event.* Some will think that since we ran a series of workshops in 1988, then in effect we've been there, done it, and don't need to do it again.

(5) *The training itself is run on a shoe-string.* Because external consultants are viewed as expensive, their skills and potential contribution are ignored and even denigrated. Further, the training events themselves don't last more than half a day, with trainers presenting to large numbers (sometimes 80 or more people) at once.

(6) *The training becomes propaganda.* Hectoring large audiences about the need for improved customer care is not likely to achieve anything at all in the way of behavioural change, no matter how professional the presentation and impressive the visual aids. It may even be counter-productive, with individuals reacting adversely to what they perceive as an insult to their intelligence.

(7) *It is thought that lecturing to people is an effective method for enhancing customer-service skills.* If reading about a skill, or listening to someone talk about a skill, were truly good ways of improving performance, then all of us could become accomplished lovers in a fairly short space of time (just as long as it takes for us to scan *The Joy of Sex*).

(8) *The training is off-the-shelf rather than custom-built.* General principles can be off-the-shelf (after all, this book is about general principles of customer care), but all generalities have to be translated into a specific context. There are genuine differences between customer-care processes in, say, hotels, financial services companies, medical practices, retail shops, software suppliers and concert halls. If employees are fed with some general (and unarguable) principles about customer care, but nobody can tell them what they are actually expected to *do* differently, then it's not surprising if they give up and simply carry on as before.

Already these difficulties suggest what has to be done to make training worthwhile.

(1) *Any customer-care programme must be linked to strategic, long-term decisions.* If it is a Pavlovian, knee-jerk, defensive reaction to initiatives elsewhere (Government intervention or competitive pressures), designed simply to give everyone the impression that the customer matters, it will soon become apparent that in reality the customer is being treated with the same contempt as before. Indeed, a customer-care programme concerned with impression-management rather than substance merely reinforces the customer-as-pawn ideology; it fools nobody and nobody benefits.

(2) *Introducing customer care is not as straightforward a process as it may seem.* We know that everyone in the organization should be devoted to their customers; some employees will claim that they are; and a few (only a few) will actually mean it. The obstacles will begin when trainers (or consultants) reveal that in fact many people are not consumer-oriented, and many organizational procedures, policies and practices are not customer-friendly. As many trainers know, trainees find it hard to assimilate any truth that violates their cherished images of themselves: so recognizing the reality of poor customer-service performance is a massive hurdle to surmount before anything else happens. Worse, trainees often don't want to accept any truths whose implications include hard work for themselves (although they don't mind if it means hard work for others).

(3) *It isn't enough to train only certain parts of the organization (for instance, by giving attention only to front-line customer-contact staff). Everything that happens inside the organization has an impact on the customer one way or another.* If front-line people are trained but nobody else, then support and back-up for these front-line people will be unchanged, and service levels will not improve. If top management

undergo a (strategic) customer-care seminar, in the hope that the message will percolate down the hierarchy of its own accord, then they are living on another planet. Such changes will be effectively scuppered by middle managers who historically have the most to lose in terms of extra work, disruption, and loss of control. So the bullet to bite is that because customer care is about culture change, the whole organization must be included in the training.

(4) *Depending on the size of the organization and the resources available, the initial training may take up to a year.* It must then be sustained and reinforced, by further workshops, brainstorming sessions and the like, plus the incorporation of a customer focus in all other relevant training exercises, especially those involving induction/indoctrination.

(5) *An imprimatur from top management is vital if the customer-care philosophy is to take off.* The imprimatur must be more than just words, because words (on the front page of a training manual, for example) are cheap. Actions, on the other hand, aren't necessarily more expensive, but they do require involvement, conscious commitment and the explicit allocation of time. During the 'Putting People First' campaign in British Airways, Sir Colin Marshall delivered the closing speech at two-thirds of the first 430 sessions. If he can do it, then so can you (or, rather, so can your CEO, if you're not there yet).

HOW TO ORGANIZE EFFECTIVE CUSTOMER-CARE TRAINING

1. Agreement on the objectives and structure of the customer-care programme as a whole

At this point the top management team has to commit itself to the required policy changes so that, in public, everyone is singing from the same hymn-sheet.

- If changes to compensation systems are required, so that people are paid by (customer-care) results, and budgets made available for one-off reward and re-cognition processes, then this is where the initiative begins.
- If the performance-appraisal procedures are to be modified so that everyone has at least one perform-ance-improvement objective related to customer care, then the change starts here.
- If the customer-care package as a whole is to be pro-moted effectively, it may need a unifying slogan, logo, and house-style: such matters should be thrashed out early on, with responsibility for im-plementation clearly allocated to the CEO or to a group that includes the CEO. In particular, the financial directorate has to be persuaded that spend-ing on customer care is a legitimate investment and not simply an optional frill.

2. An audit of the current situation

It is commonplace to conduct two attitude surveys, one covering employees (with such questions as 'What would a customer find most unsettling about business with me?') and the second covering customers. The purpose of the audit is to check whether initial assess-ments of the nature and scope of the 'problem' are accu-rate. All too often they are not, because senior manage-ment is deluded, or deludes itself, or because customers have never been asked for their views before, or because internal departments have never asked their customers for reactions before.

3. Workshops to plan the customer-care programme in greater depth

These workshops can develop into team-building exer-cises, since they are typically structured around cohe-rent units like departments, sections, production groups or regional sales teams. However, they can also point up causes of frustration for which straightforward remedies are available (without the need for training), ranging from the way the work is organized to ergonomic problems with equipment (uncomfortable chairs or inadequate lighting).

It is vital that the workshops acquire and sustain a problem-solving focus. Group therapy (the ritual blaming of others) is just about acceptable at the beginning, but as a way of life it has its limitations. Far preferable is a constructive approach based on the implications of the internal and external attitude surveys, concentrating on the key question: *How can we make sure we get better scores when we do these surveys next time?*

4. Implementation of new policies and objectives

We're still not yet at the point where the training begins, because the training is just part of a multi-pronged attack on the customer-care issues. As an example of the type of change to be introduced, the personnel function may have to alter its recruitment criteria so that customer-service orientation becomes a requirement for all jobs, rather than simply for jobs involving direct contact with external customers. All departments and functions may need to introduce customer care as a leading agenda item for their team meetings.

5. An internal publicity campaign

This will prepare the ground for the overall culture change and also, more specifically, for the training programme. The launch of a customer-care drive is a marketing issue, very much like any other product or service launch, so why not engage the services of your marketing department? The launch itself must generate a massive impact, so if resources are skimped then the campaign will fizzle out almost before it's begun. All the organization's communication media have to be exploited: newsletters, company magazines, bulletins from the CEO, video presentations, roadshows, noticeboard displays, giveaways (inscribed coffee mugs), PC 'commercials', and so forth. A couple of points are worth emphasizing about the publicity:

- *It* **must** *say, and keep repeating, that this is an organization-wide responsibility.* It isn't just a management game. If people think it is, many will conclude that customer care is something for 'them' and nothing to do with 'us'.
- *Right from the start, the publicity must give some information on how everyone will become involved.* It's not enough to offer platitudes about the opportunity for participating: specific mechanisms have to be developed.
- *People have to learn what's in it for them.* Why should they adopt customer–care behaviour patterns, if they've got on very well without them in the past? How will such behaviour change be reinforced, recognized and rewarded?
- *It doesn't motivate your staff to say that the organization has to become more customer-friendly if it is to stay in business.* Some employees will think they are already friendly enough; some will think it doesn't apply to them; some quite simply won't believe the implied threats (they'll say they've heard it all before); some won't care, on the grounds that they're near retirement anyway and if the organization goes under they think they will be better off.
- *Motivating people by fear (you have to change because if you don't you'll be out of a job) is no way to generate customer-service improvements from an enthusiastic and committed workforce.* During Phase Five, the organization has to review every aspect of its systems that will help to maintain the impetus after the initial training sessions and publicity campaign have been completed. For example: how can the 'product life cycle' for customer–care be extended?

The Customer-care training programme itself.
What follows is a list of some of the crucial issues concerned with the training design, and some suggested solutions.
How should the groups be structured?
There are two main schools of thought on how the training should be structured. The first argues that employees should be divided into 'streams', with separate sessions for senior managers, middle managers, supervisors and so forth, generally on a cross-functional basis. The case for 'streaming' is strengthened if difficult messages need to be put across to different levels of management. Moreover, if senior managers undergo the training first, as part of a cascade pattern, and begin putting it into practice, this will reinforce the subsequent training for those at lower levels.

The other option is 'vertical slicing', with all levels of staff attending the same course. The advantage here is that people not in regular contact with customers have a better chance to see their job in the context of the total picture. Vertical slicing promotes team cohesion within functions, but this can be dangerous if it does nothing to undermine inter-departmental rivalries (it may even exacerbate them).

In reality, most organizations (and especially larger ones) offer opportunities for a mixture of streamed and vertically sliced training groups. Streaming works best if the delegates already have links with each other through a customer-service supply chain so that, in a sense, they have a common identity. Vertical slicing operates successfully, for instance, if the groups comprise everyone from the same branch, division or unit, within organizations where each segment has relatively little to do with its counterparts. In a building society, for example, it does not particularly matter if individual branches develop a competitive rivalry between themselves; but it would be different if supposedly co-operating departments within corporate HQ started to become even more insular.

Need we use consultants?

One key question is whether consultants should be engaged to lead the training sessions, or whether the sessions should be organized internally. As is usual in debates of this kind, the 'right' decision does not leap unambiguously out of the woodwork. External consultants may (though not always) have higher credibility by virtue of their breadth of experience and (if you're cynical) the fees they charge; internal trainers have less chance of making an impact simply because they are prophets in their own land.

Given the fact that a customer-care programme is about culture change, such significant shifts of direction can only be signalled if there is extensive and active involvement by senior management from inside the organization, perhaps reinforced by the presence of properly briefed consultants. Yet for consultants to undertake all the training, whether the focus is strategic (for senior levels) or operational (for front-line staff), can make people think that the organization is only playing with the idea of customer service. It looks as if management is standing on the sidelines, waiting to see what will happen, ready to jump either way if customer care turns out to be a bandwagon worth riding or a hearse on its way to the crematorium.

On the other hand, if all the training is led by in-house trainers and the organization's own management, there is a danger it will be introspective, incestuous and even complacent. It might not be all that professional, either, although this can be counteracted if participating managers receive some jump-start guidance on presentation skills and techniques.

Consultants are certainly well placed to carry out some specific activities in the run-up to customer-care training, such as attitude surveys; they can act as helpful facilitators for the planning phase, both at strategic and tactical levels. The fact that consultants have under-taken the research necessary for the attitude surveys adds to their credibility as trainers, of course, when it comes to using customer feedback as targeted ammuni-tion in the training sessions. In choosing a consultancy, a simple approach is to identify organizations whose level of service is consistently impressive and find out which consultancies they employed. Another simple test is to look at the level of service that consultancies themselves provide at the initial point of contact. Such a test can be very illuminating. The author's own con-sultancy business has frequently benefited indirectly from the offhand behaviour of competitors. We're told that their telephonists can be unhelpful, their staff can be patronizing, their responses can be slow, their pro-posals can be clearly off-the-shelf despite claims about being tailor-made, and some of their information (espe-cially about expenses) is hard to extract. Without blow-ing the trumpet for The PROSPER Consortium too much, we take the view that if we're preaching the vir-tues of positive customer service, we have to live by the behaviour we expect from our clients.

What about the numbers to be trained at any one time?

There are differing views on the optimum size for train-ing groups. Of course, the budget can be a vital factor, but to say this is to imply that a budget is a fixed alloca-tion of resources when in reality it is not. On the contrary, the size of the budget available for the customer-care programme is itself indicative of the seriousness with which the whole thing is being approached.

Another constraint is time. For large organizations there may be no alternative to using large groups if the aim is to compete the initial programme quickly. In the case of British Airways, 36,524 staff went through the initial 'Putting People First' series, which ran continuously between November 1983 and June 1985. There was an average attendance of 140 participants at each session. Other organizations have decided to train 80 or more delegates at a single occasion, arguing that in large groups the participants come to see themselves as part of a whole organization, to understand the effect they have on others, and to appreciate the importance of shelving inter-departmental conflicts.

We regard such propositions as specious. So-called 'training' with such large groups is not training at all, but a religious revival meeting.

- It may be inspirational (but only if imaginatively led)
- It may cause some people to suspend their belief (but not for long)
- It may be cheap (but not cost-effective).

Presentations in front of conference-size audiences will inevitably dwell largely on rhetoric, sweeping generalities and emotional appeals – all very well in their place, but not much use if you're a counter clerk, a delivery driver, or a hotel receptionist, and you want to know what you're expected to *do* differently. By all means set the scene with the flag-waving, messianic roadshow; but it has to be followed closely and immediately by smaller-scale workshops to answer the single significant question (if you're at the sharp end): *How do we make it happen?*

The argument for smaller groups, in any case, is that they allow individual participation. In larger groups, only the more extrovert employees really become involved and there is no chance to answer the legitimate objections of people who, inhibited already, become even more inhibited when asked to open their mouths in front of 80, or even 140 others. With smaller groups it is possible to get through to each person on a powerful emotional level. Above all, smaller groups permit genuine *skills training* to be undertaken, with a mixture of conceptual inputs, role-play exercises, performance feedback and action-plan development. Small groups encourage genuine team-building, especially if the groups themselves comprise people from connected functions or from one geographical location – and it becomes easier to build on the training afterwards through action workshops and the like, simply because everyone has undergone the same shared experience from the outset.

How do we know if it has done any good?
Customer-care programmes are notoriously difficult to evaluate quantitatively. One obvious measure is a 'before and after' study of the level of customer complaints. This approach was taken by Pizza Hut, which found that service-related complaints fell by half in the year after their formal customer-care programme had been initiated; this was matched by triple the number of written customer compliments. Pizza Hut concedes that it is not possible to attribute this exclusively to its customer-care efforts, but at least the indicators were pointing in the right direction.

It's worth remembering, however, that if you make it public that your organization has gone through a customer-care programme, customer expectations are increased. What may happen is that your organization receives more complaints, even though standards have risen.

Initially this can be depressing, to put it mildly. It is especially depressing if there are no measures of performance other than customer feedback, because you won't know that your standards have (objectively) gone up: all you'll know is that you're getting more complaints. You could deduce that your performance has deteriorated and you'll have nothing other than impressionistic evidence to persuade you that this isn't the case. If you *know* that your delivery times are faster, or your product quality is better, but you're receiving more brickbats, then you can see what is happening more clearly. You still have to do something about it, of course. At least your customers are complaining rather than simply going elsewhere.

TYPICAL TRAINING PROGRAMMES
It's a mistake to start at the bottom. The customer-service message has to be absorbed from the top downwards if anything significant is to happen.

Senior management
With senior managers, the purpose of the training is to provide awareness, demonstrate the commercial/survival benefits of positive/customer care, gain commitment, and secure undertakings of visible endorsement for the continuing exercise. Given these overall objectives, then a senior management training session (it's often better to call it a 'seminar' rather than a 'course' or even a 'workshop' so far as senior people are concerned) may contain these elements:

(1) *What 'customer care' is about*: with references to both internal and external customers, and the customer-service supply chain. The distinction between 'customers' and 'users' may be significant here.
(2) *The commercial/survival benefits to be gained from a strategic focus on positive customer care*: examples of conspicuous successes and notorious disasters.
(3) *Evaluation of the attitude survey results*: related to both internal and external customers.
(4) *Agreement on the principal objectives for the organization's customer care programme.*

(5) *Development of customer-oriented mission and vision statements*: or adaptation of the current statements if some already exist.

(6) *What it means in practice*: turning some high-sounding principles into practical action will involve discussion on systems, procedures, delegation of responsibility and authority to front-line staff, the role of senior managers in setting and sustaining the impetus, and so forth.

(7) *Overcoming the barriers to change*: the principal objections to a customer-care focus and how they can be addressed.

(8) *Methods for generating ownership throughout the organization*: especially at front-line levels, through coaching, leadership, and appropriate reward/recognition systems.

(9) *Production of agreed Action Plans for policy, strategic, tactical and individual implementation.*

Especially significant in all this is the need to secure public statements from the participating senior managers about their personal involvement with the customer-care initiative and the specific behaviour changes they will introduce in order to help the programme on its way.

The role of the trainer is to facilitate, rather than lay down the law, as it were. What should happen is that peer pressure will shift the opinions of those who don't currently display the required leadership priorities or customer-care orientation.

Middle management

Critical to the success of any customer-care adventure is the behaviour of middle management, since they are often the focal point of any resistance to change. Much of the content of any training programme for middle managers will depend on whether there is already a strong training and development culture embedded in the organization. If there is, managers may already be equipped with professional presentation skills (which they will need in order to deliver customer-service information to their staff), team-building processes, leadership techniques, meeting management and discussion leading, brainstorming and other methods for encouraging creativity across the board. If there isn't a training/development culture, then competence in these management techniques has to be addressed, as well as:

(1) *The meaning of customer care*: defining the 'customer' and the 'user' both within the organization and to the outside world.
(2) *The urgent need for positive action to implement customer-care initiatives*: for competitive advantage, for improved results, for survival.
(3) *Detailed discussion of any previous attitude survey results*: concentrating on the implications for middle managers themselves.
(4) *Translating the mission and vision statement into everyday behaviour for the middle manager.*
(5) *Overcoming the barriers to change*: creating 'ownership' for customer care.
(6) *Techniques for making it happen down the line*: the role of the manager in general terms, amplified into specific tools for leadership, communication, team-building, delegation (empowerment), involvement through performance improvement and innovation.
(7) *Public commitment to individual Action Plans for change.*

Direct-contact customer-service people

At the front-line customer-service level, we can concentrate on staff who have continuous exposure to customers. Although at first sight it may seem sensible to target these staff first, in fact it's essential, if the training is to be effective, for:

- *Managers to be involved* in the development of the programme
- *Managers to participate* actively in the programme (not just sit at the back); and
- *Managers to be seen to make changes* as a consequence of the training they have received. (This is called leadership by example.)

In the 1980s it was fashionable for training aimed at front-line staff to have an evangelical flavour: polished and professional presentations leading to passion, excitement and (hopefully) performance. The major disadvantage of this type of 'training' (if we can call it that) is that the presenter cannot be certain that everyone is involved and taking the messages on board, as it were. The effectiveness of evangelical training depends strongly on endorsement of the learning process by individual managers after the participants have returned to the workplace – and this support is often lacking.

A more exploratory approach will take groups of customer-service staff and relate the general principles of customer care to the context of their work, taking actual examples to illustrate the process in action. A typical workshop for front-line people will display a strong *skills development* focus – much more so than similar workshops for senior and middle managers – and may include:

(1) *An explanation of why the organization is taking action on customer care*: why such action is important (not only to the organization but, more significantly, why it's important for the front-line staff now being trained).
(2) *Inputs about the expectations of our customers*: based on

attitude surveys and other evidence; how well we currently meet those expectations; how these expectations may change in the foreseeable future; and how a customer-care orientation means a radical shift in attitudes and behaviour from everyone.

(3) *Ways of improving performance:* through face-to-face contact with customers, telephone communications, written/fax media, complaint-handling procedures.

(4) *Practical work to enhance relevant skills*: face-to-face communication, assertiveness, influence and persuasion skills, questioning and information-gathering, positive body language, and the like.

(5) *Specification of attainable performance standards in appropriate arenas of customer care*: response times, waiting times, complaint reductions, zero-defect targets, or positive customer reactions.

(6) *Agreement and commitment to the proposed changes*: including a clear statement about the tangible benefits to the individuals concerned (through appropriate reward and recognition systems).

Making It Happen

As with any other training exercise, maximum psychological pressures have to be applied in order to increase the likelihood that personal Action Plans are translated into meaningful results. These pressures can encompass:

(1) *Personal Action Plan presentations by each participant*: based on a strong brief that prevents the inclusion of generalized platitudes.

(2) *Delivery of Action Plan presentations in the presence of the CEO* or some other crucial driver for customer-care in the organization.

(3) *Transmission of Action Plan documents to each participant's senior manager*: with a specific requirement

for further discussion, elaboration of key points, and agreement about further follow-up.

(4) *Absorption of individual Action Plan commitments into subsequent performance appraisal procedures.*

(5) *Systematic evaluation of Action Plan promises*: to ensure that results are delivered.

(6) *Creation of highly visible reward systems*: for recognizing progress, improvement and performance.

(7) *Continuous monitoring of feedback from 'customers' for each delegate.*

Obviously the precise content of any training programme – whether aimed at senior management, middle managers or front-line staff – has to be directed towards the operating circumstances of the client organization. At the front-line level, for example, virtually everyone can benefit from communication-skills training in such areas as listening, questioning, giving clear explanations, summarizing and problem-solving. In some organizations, however, handling telephone calls will be the major issue. For others it will be face-to-face transactions with customers that count more than anything. Within white collar bureaucracies it may make sense to concentrate on written communications because there is little direct personal interface with customers. Of course, another, more lateral-thinking solution is actually to increase the opportunity for direct contact with customers, instead of confining ourselves solely to performance improvements within the status quo.

WHAT ELSE IS NEEDED?

Everyone knows that training has to be reinforced if it is to 'take'.

That's why customer-care initiatives have to start at the top. Even then it won't be enough. Mobilizing continuous action requires constant repackaging of the 'product', otherwise people will become complacent. They will assume that because the massive training exercise has finished, customer care can now be forgotten, especially if there is evidence of improved achievement (from another batch of attitude survey forms). Customer care was 'flavour of the month' but has been replaced by something else, it will be said.

Even the phrase 'customer care' is beginning to have an old-fashioned 'yesterday' feel about it (just like the term 'excellence', which was compulsorily on every manager's lips in the late 1980s, but which now brands you indelibly as an old fogey). So it's better to think up other titles in the first place. Roget's *Thesaurus* is a handy source of ideas. Then you have to keep the momentum going. This can be done through driving forward the apparatus associated with customer care:

(1) *Re-training everyone involved after a year or so* (which will also enable newcomers to catch up): a product relaunch with new labels, new performance expectations, new forms of customer feedback, new levels of empowerment, new ways of keeping ahead of the competition (or reacting to it).
(2) *Constantly rewarding and celebrating progress, performance and achievement at every level of the organization and in every part of its operation*: plus new ways of rewarding people, to keep interest alive.
(3) *Retaining customer-care enhancement as an integral part of performance appraisal*: with the obligation that at least one objective for the next review period will focus on service development.
(4) *Incorporation of customer-care issues into regular team-meetings*: especially at board level, so that the message cascades downwards.
(5) *Continued requirement for senior and middle-level staff to devote an agreed percentage of their time to their customers (or to the organization's customers)*.

(6) *Well-publicized modifications to relevant systems, policies and procedures*: in order to make them even more user and customer friendly. There's no reason why this effort should ever end.

(7) *Exposure of the organization's practices to external scrutiny*: via consultants, professional bodies or quality-standards institutions.

(8) *Regular studies of the outside world*: undertaken by small teams of managers temporarily seconded from their current roles, briefed to uncover what can be learned, copied, adapted or improved from ideas pioneered by others. (Note that these 'others' shouldn't only include direct competitors: you may develop significant customer-service changes for, say, your accountancy business by watching McDonalds in action. To be snooty about other organizations because they, or we, are 'different' is to close off potentially exciting opportunities for competitive advantage.)

(9) *Frequent communications of key messages through all the media available*: noticeboards, posters, the fax machine, PCs, newsletters, company newspapers, press releases, video, corporate reports.

(10) *Reiteration of the customer-care philosophy on all internal and external documents used by the organization*: invoices, letter-heads, memo-pads, telephone message notes, delivery documents, the sides of vehicles, order forms, namestands used by course participants, supporting notes, telephone directories, instruction manuals, expense forms (this is the one everybody will read!) and restaurant menus.

One word of warning: with all these devices, a zero-defect performance standard is obligatory. If you harangue others on the need to improve performance, and then make a mess of it as you do so, you will never recover. Your credibility will be shot to hell, and what's worse, you'll deserve it.

8

WHY YOU'VE GOT TO DO IT AND KEEP ON DOING IT

The simple answer is that if you don't you're doomed.

You may represent an organization which is already in the vanguard for customer care: you may even work for one of the paradigms, the exemplars, the Marks & Spencers of this world. Even for you, life isn't easy. Give customers more and they want more still. You can't afford to hang about. You certainly shouldn't assume that further improvement is impossible. There will always be someone generating new approaches, new customer benefits, new standards of performance.

If you're not in the vanguard, things are much worse. You're falling behind. Cost control becomes more difficult, yet you need to spend in order to hang on to what you've got in a competitive environment where others set the pace.

Some may argue that all this talk about customers and customer care is a passing phase. Soon we'll get over it, just as we passed through the vale of human relations, of job enrichment, of excellence and participation. Keep your head down, goes the argument, and eventually we'll be able to carry on as before, treating customers as if they should be grateful to be able to buy our products or use our services, and if they don't like it they can go somewhere else.

It's a possible though very improbable scenario. This obsession with customers may eventually fade into the background, but by the time it does many organizations will have achieved a quantum leap in customer-service standards. If you've stayed where you were before, you'll be even further behind.

Moreover, if customer care recedes into the middle distance, that doesn't mean we stop thinking about it. The search for sustainable competitive advantage must continue, and customers will play a pivotal role in contributing to that search.

Don't forget that ultimately it is customers who pay for the work we do. Without customers there is no work to be done. Without readers there are no books to be written, so these pages will be rapidly remaindered.

There are still plenty of organizations with much to learn about customer care. We've seen that readily enough from the horror stories told in earlier chapters. Even Marks & Spencer is not infallible: it took ages to supply changing rooms and, like many other retailers, it still doesn't put complementary products close to each other. If Marks & Spencer isn't perfect, then think about:

(1) Organizations that recognize they have customers, and have to compete for them, but still don't make any systematic effort to find out what their customers think about what they do, or what their customers might want;

(2) Organizations that are in a competitive marketplace but have yet to recognize it;

(3) Organizations that have customers who are tied to them and who therefore have no choice, like local authorities, the National Health Service, government departments;

(4) Organizations that talk the language of customer care but whose actions indicate continuing indifference, apathy and even contempt;

(5) Organizations that don't even acknowledge the existence of customers.

You could be in one of these categories. Fortunately

some latecomers are reluctantly accepting the logic of customer care. Just recently the *Daily Telegraph* reported that in the classical concert business, the people who have to sell the seats are thinking for the first time about looking after their customers. The South Bank complex in London is preparing to replace its house managers (whose previous obsessions have focused on neat and tidy administration) with customer-service specialists working to specifications copied from international airlines. All front-of-house staff are being retrained to smile, hold doors open and thank you for flying Mozart.

Why is this happening? The answer is simple:

- Most concert-goers are aged over 50, and are not being replaced by the younger generation
- The Royal Festival Hall plays, on nightly average, at below two-thirds of its 2,900 seat capacity
- The product itself (the music) has made no concession to changing tastes. The overture, concerto and symphony format is virtually invariable
- Start times and finish times are determined by what is convenient for the musicians, not the audience
- The performers' attitude to the customers is condescending: eye contact is non-existent, for example.

Note that even here the pressure for improved customer care has come from the bottom line. It hasn't come from any initiative by imaginative, entrepreneurial concert-hall managers or orchestra directors. Curious, is it not? Well, no, it's not; actually it's rather typical, and at the same time sad, that it takes people voting with their feet before some individuals recognize that the world has changed.

When we get to the point where everyday life embraces

these choices and opportunities, we shall know that customer care is embedded into organizational cultures:

- You ring up the Barbican to book for a Colin Davis concert; you're told that your favourite seats, T22 and T23 are available, and your complimentary drinks will be waiting at the Level 5 bar in the interval. You're also asked if you will require crèche facilities for your two children, as usual
- As an NHS patient, you're given a specific appointment time for your hospital visit; you're invited to select your preferred date for your prostate operation
- The local authority processes your planning application within two weeks (with the aim of reducing it to ten days next year)
- Your insurance company sends out bonus statements and pension calculations printed in a manner that enables you to understand them immediately
- Hotels offer you a discount if you complete and return their guest questionnaires; you also get a personalized response from the managing director
- Banks produce their financial charges using large print rather than small. Further, they only send you details of the charges that apply to you
- Application forms for bank accounts make it sound as if they'll be pleased to have you as a customer
- Product brochures tell you what the product will do for you, rather than how it works.

APPENDIX A

OUTLINE CUSTOMER QUALITY SERVICE QUESTIONNAIRE

The following will give some ideas on what can be done with a simple customer-service questionnaire. Obviously there is no suggestion that you should simply copy out these questions and use them as they stand: some may not be at all appropriate to your needs, and most will have to be modified. However, the questionnaire can be adapted to fit either internal or external customers, or could be targeted towards specific categories of customer.

CUSTOMER QUALITY SURVEY

We appreciate your business and want to continue providing high-quality products/services which meet (or preferably more than meet) your requirements. We would also like to do it on time. Please answer the following questions to assist us in our efforts to maintain high quality standards.

Rating scale: 1 = lowest score 5 = highest score

	Importance to you	Your rating of our performance
1. Responsiveness to your needs	5 4 3 2 1	5 4 3 2 1
2. Delivery of our product/ service	5 4 3 2 1	5 4 3 2 1
3. Speed of service	5 4 3 2 1	5 4 3 2 1
4. Willingness to change to meet your changing needs	5 4 3 2 1	5 4 3 2 1
5. Face-to-fact interaction	5 4 3 2 1	5 4 3 2 1
6. Telephone interaction	5 4 3 2 1	5 4 3 2 1
7. Quality of follow-up service	5 4 3 2 1	5 4 3 2 1

What two things could we do to measurably improve our quality so far as you are concerned?

1. _____

2. _____

Additional topics for coverage within your customer-service studies could include (especially if you're responsible for a product as opposed to a service) the adequacy of the product itself, its design, packaging, assembly/use instructions, and so forth. Don't forget that it's desirable to talk with a few customers before putting your questionnaire together, in order to get ideas for appropriate themes and issues. Also any questionnaire must be pilot-tested before going out to its target population: only in this way can you protect yourself against indefensible errors in question design, layout, grammar, punctuation and even spelling.

APPENDIX B

CUSTOMER SERVICE CHECKLIST

Customer Education

1. Are product/service usage/assembly instructions clearly and precisely given? YES NO

2. Is customer understanding of instructions monitored regularly? YES NO

3. Do actual/potential customers know the extent of service back-up available? YES NO

4. Do PR and media activities inform customers of all product/service benefits? YES NO

5. Do the public at large know of your organization and its products/services? YES NO

6. Do the public think that the organization cares? YES NO

If each question can be answered Yes, OK. If No, do something.

Staff Selection and Training

7. Do recruitment and selection criteria specifically emphasise the need for *all* staff to have helpful, pro-customer attitudes? YES NO

8. Do selection procedures include customer-orientation questions on application forms? YES NO

9. At selection interviews, are candidates asked about their experiences with customers and judged accordingly? YES NO

10. Is there an induction programme for new employees?   YES   NO
11. Does the induction programme include a strong emphasis on customer care (as opposed to technical knowledge)?   YES   NO
12. Is there specific staff training in telephone techniques?   YES   NO
13. Are staff trained for face-to-face meetings with their customers and/or the public?   YES   NO
14. Do customer needs take priority over in-house organization activities?   YES   NO
15. Is management action taken when employee irritation with customers is identified?   YES   NO
16. Is there specific staff training in the PR implications of employee conduct?   YES   NO
17. Do front-line staff like their customers?   YES   NO
18. Do staff know about customer levels of expectation?   YES   NO
19. Are there specific incentives to motivate front-line staff?   YES   NO
20. Do they have job satisfaction?   YES   NO

If each question can be answered Yes, OK. If No, do something.

Customer Complaints Administration

21. Is there a policy regarding customer complaints?   YES   NO
22. Is there a standardized complaint response procedure?   YES   NO
23. Are complaints procedure documents used for customer complaints calls?   YES   NO
24. Are complaints recorded?   YES   NO

25. Are complaints analysed regularly for management action? YES NO
26. Have the problems of complaint categories over six months old been resolved? YES NO
27. Are staff sympathetic towards customer complaint problems? YES NO
28. Have staff been trained to deal with angry customers? YES NO
29. Is management action taken when customer irritation with employees is identified? YES NO

If each question can be answered Yes, OK. If No, do something.

Customer Feedback

30. Is there a regular system for securing systematic customer feedback? YES NO
31. Does the method use proper sampling techniques? YES NO
32. If using a questionnaire, does it offer customers the opportunity to give feedback on every aspect of the product/service? YES NO
33. Does the questionnaire include explanations from the CEO (or equivalent)? YES NO
34. Does the questionnaire have to be returned to a named individual (preferably the CEO)? YES NO
35. Are incentives offered to encourage customers to give feedback (e.g. rewards for completing a questionnaire)? YES NO
36. Is favourable feedback solicited, for example, when instances of customer 'delight' are experienced? YES NO

37. When systematic customer feedback is obtained, are the results published within the organization? YES NO
38. Are the results published in the outside world, e.g., for the benefit of customers? YES NO
39. Are especially strenuous efforts made to secure feedback from ex-customers? YES NO

If each question can be answered Yes, OK. If No, do something.

Internal Customers

40. Do you (and your colleagues or staff) willingly acknowledge that you have customers inside your organization? YES NO
41. Do you know who they are? YES NO
42. Do you regularly seek to improve your service to these customers, whether they've asked for it or not? YES NO
43. Do you seek to test-market new services to your existing customers, again whether they've asked for them or not? YES NO
44. Do you conduct brainstorming sessions in conjunction with your internal customers in order to develop service improvements and/or new services for them? YES NO
45. Do you seek to extend your services to new internal customers? YES NO
46. Are there any possibilities for supplying your services to external customers as well? YES NO
47. Do you adequately publicize your customer-oriented activities so that other internal departments can learn from your example? YES NO

If each question can be answered Yes, OK, If No, do something.

FURTHER READING

Cook, Sarah *Customer Care – Implementing Total Quality in Today's Service-Driven Organisation*. London: Kogan Page, 1992.

Freemantle, David *Incredible Customer Service – The Final Test*. Maidenhead: McGraw–Hill, 1993.

Tunks, Roger *Fast Track to Quality – A 12-month Program for Small to Mid-Sized Businesses*. New York: McGraw–Hill, 1992.

Linton, Ian *Building Customer Loyalty*. London: Pitman Publishing, 1993.

Chaston, Ian *Customer-Focused Marketing – Actions for Delivering Greater Internal and External Customer Satisfaction*. Maidenhead: McGraw–Hill, 1993.

Katz, Bernard *How to Turn Customer Service into Customer Sales*. Aldershot: Wildwood House, 1988.

Hammer, Michael, and Champy, James *Re-Engineering the Corporation – A Manifesto for Business Revolution*. London: Nicholas Brearley Publishing, 1993.